Before the Law

Before the Law

HUMANS AND OTHER ANIMALS IN A BIOPOLITICAL FRAME

Cary Wolfe

The University of Chicago Press :: Chicago and London

Cary Wolfe is chair and the Bruce and Elizabeth Dunlevie Professor in the Department of English at Rice University. His books include *What Is Posthumanism?* and *Animal Rites: American Culture, the Discourse of Species, and Posthumanist Theory*, the latter also published by the University of Chicago Press.

The University of Chicago Press, Chicago 60637
The University of Chicago Press, Ltd., London
© 2013 by The University of Chicago
All rights reserved. Published 2013.
Printed in the United States of America

22 21 20 19 18 17 16 15 14 13   1 2 3 4 5

ISBN-13: 978-0-226-92240-9 (cloth)
ISBN-13: 978-0-226-92241-6 (paper)
ISBN-13: 978-0-226-92242-3 (e-book)
ISBN-10: 0-226-92240-5 (cloth)
ISBN-10: 0-226-92241-3 (paper)
ISBN-10: 0-226-92242-1 (e-book)

Portions of this book first appeared in an article titled "Before the Law: Animals in a Biopolitical Context," *Law, Culture, and the Humanities* 6, no. 1 (2010): 8–23.

Library of Congress Cataloging-in-Publication Data

Wolfe, Cary.
  Before the law : humans and other animals in a biopolitical
frame / Cary Wolfe.
    pages. cm.
  Includes bibliographical references and index.
  ISBN-13: 978-0-226-92240-9 (cloth : alk. paper)
  ISBN-10: 0-226-92240-5 (cloth : alk. paper)
  ISBN-13: 978-0-226-92241-6 (pbk. : alk. paper)
  ISBN-10: 0-226-92241-3 (pbk. : alk. paper)
  [etc.]
  1. Animal rights—Moral and ethical aspects. 2. Animal
rights—Political aspects. 3. Animal rights—Economic aspects.
4. Speciesism. I. Title.
  HV4708.W654 2013
  179'.3—dc23

2012019260

♾ This paper meets the requirements of ANSI/NISO Z39.48-1992 (Permanence of Paper).

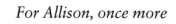

For Allison, once more

Contents

Before the Law

I.

To begin at the beginning: I choose the word "frame" for my title (rather than adjacent terms such as, say, "context") for a few different reasons that interconnect some of the subterranean conceptual passageways of this long essay. First, I want to mark a lengthening genealogy of biopolitical thought that stretches back from current avatars such as Roberto Esposito, Judith Butler, and Giorgio Agamben through the *locus classicus* of Michel Foucault's later work (a *locus* that is becoming more and more *classicus* by the day, thanks to the ongoing translation and publication of his lectures at the Collège de France), to what we are now in a position to see as biopolitical thought *avant la lettre*, as it were, in the work of Hannah Arendt and Martin Heidegger. Directly pertinent for my title is the sense of Heidegger's *Gestell* ("enframing" or "framework," as it is often translated) from his well-known later essay, "The Question Concerning Technology."[1] There, Heidegger asserts that the essence of technology is not "anything technological" but rather how it discloses the world to us as a mode of "bringing-forth" what is here for us, and how.[2] For Heidegger (and, as we shall see, for biopolitical thought generally), enframing is anything but a neutral concept; indeed, with the luxury of twenty-twenty hindsight, we can now see that it is deep background (as the journalists say) for what Foucault and others will call the *dispositifs* or apparatuses of biopolitics. *Gestell*, while neither natural nor human, frames the human's relation both to itself and to nature, and in ways that are far from sanguine in Heidegger's view.[3] "Where enframing reigns," Heidegger writes, "there is *danger* in the highest sense."[4] What we encounter here is a mode of revealing the world which sets it out before us in a mode of instrumentality and

locus classicus

:: 3

utility that Heidegger famously calls "standing-reserve" (*Bestand*). As Heidegger puts it in a well-known passage,

> As soon as what is unconcealed no longer concerns man even as object, but does so, rather, exclusively as standing-reserve, and man in the midst of objectlessness is nothing but the orderer of the standing reserve, then he comes to the brink of a precipitous fall; that is, he comes to the point where he himself will have to be taken as standing-reserve. Meanwhile man, precisely as the one so threatened, exalts himself to the posture of lord of the earth. In this way the impression comes to prevail that everything man encounters exists only insofar as it is his construct. This illusion gives rise to one final delusion: It seems as though man everywhere and always encounters only himself.[5]

But the self he encounters is, as Heidegger notes, fallen, inauthentic: "*In truth, however,*" Heidegger continues, "*precisely nowhere does man today any longer encounter himself, i.e. his essence.*"[6]

The effect of this enframing is thus twofold: not only are human beings cut off from a more authentic relation to the natural world, they are also cut off from an authentic relationship to themselves. Sounding notes that, as we'll see, both Michel Foucault and Peter Sloterdijk will amplify decades later, Heidegger asserts that humanity thus comes, in fact, to be seen as a kind of standing-reserve in and of itself—a fact reflected in the contemporary reframing of individuals as "human resources" and the like.[7] Over and against this work of *Gestell*, Heidegger sets what he calls the "saving power"[8] of a humanity (and a humanism) not wholly subordinated to calculation and utility, one that is able to engage artistically, poetically, and philosophically, in reflection and meditation, in questioning (hence Derrida's emphasis in the subtitle of his book on Heidegger, *Of Spirit*, on Heidegger and "*the question*").[9]

We find here, then, not just one of the high-water marks of humanism's familiar opposition of art and philosophy, on the one hand, to calculation and utility, on the other, but also an even deeper and more decisive determination of the proper and improper relation of the human to technology, and hence to itself: "Technology is no mere means," Heidegger reminds us, and while it may operate improperly as calculation and resource management, it may also take on a more edifying role in "the arts of the mind and the fine arts," where it "belongs to bringing-forth, to *poiesis.*"[10] In fact, as Heidegger's thought develops in both "The Question Concerning Technology" and the "Letter on Humanism," this difference between a proper and improper relationship to technology enables, in turn, a decisive ontological distinction between those who are fully human and those who are less than human, those others who have been so fundamentally distanced from Being by an improper relationship to technology that their very humanity is in question.[11] As Heidegger writes in the "Letter," "For this is humanism: meditating and caring, that man be human and not inhumane, 'inhuman,' that is, outside his essence."[12]

Now we know, as I have pointed out elsewhere (following well-known discussions by Derrida and others), that the primary means by which this "saving" takes place is above all through the capacity for language, which is, properly understood, not semiotic but phenomenological, and gives access to things "as such," as opposed to language understood as "communication," "information," and the like.[13] We thus find a fundamental distinction, as Timothy Campbell puts it, "between those, on one side who are mere subjects of communication; those who later will be enrolled among the ranks of *animalitas*; and others who, thanks to a proper writing, are seen as free, individual human beings, capable of 'care.'"[14] Precisely here, in this distinction between the proper and improper relation not just to technology but more fundamentally of the human to itself, we may locate the hinge in Heidegger's work between the two main lines of contemporary biopolitical thought, one (associated with Foucault) focused on technology and *dispositifs,* and the other (associated with Agamben) focused on the subject's proper relation to its own singularity and uniqueness—its "ipseity" (to use the term Derrida will later unpack in relation to the question of sovereignty). By these lights, ipseity and sovereignty are taken to be in stark opposition to the "animal,"[15] and to the animality of the human when the human becomes something anonymous, either through massification (as in Foucault's studies of the mechanisms of biopolitics, such as population sciences and medicalization) or by being reduced to an equally anonymous condition of "bare life."[16] But what I want to emphasize here is Heidegger's opening up of a gap—a dangerous gap, as the history of biopolitics

personal identity

well shows, but also one jealously guarded by humanism—between humanity and animality as ontologically opposed zones. Indeed, the "humans *and other animals*" of my title is meant as a direct challenge to this distinction, so crucial to Heidegger's entire corpus—indeed, one of its central dogmas (to use Derrida's characterization[17]).

Heidegger's meditations on the frame and enframing will eventually be radicalized and pushed to their self-deconstructing conclusions in another famous discussion of the frame—namely, Derrida's analysis of the *parergon* (a term he borrows from Kant) as that "which simultaneously constitutes and destroys" what it frames, paradoxically supplementing that which is already complete.[18] It separates the inside from the outside, the intrinsic and the extrinsic, and yet also serves to bridge them, making them interdependent. Derrida's analysis of the *parergon* does to Heidegger's *Gestell* what his *pharmakon* will do to Heidegger's distinction between the proper and the improper—and in ways, as we will see, that connect directly to what Roberto Esposito and others have identified as the "immunitary" (and, with Derrida, "autoimmunitary") logic of the biopolitical.[19] To put it this way is to remind ourselves that the question of framing is not simply a logical or epistemological problem but a social and material one, with consequences. Framing decides what we recognize and what we don't, what counts and what doesn't; and it also determines the consequences of falling outside the frame (in the case at hand, outside the frame as "animal," as "*zoe*," as "bare life").

We are now in a better position to critically assess, however briefly, another towering figure in the prehistory of contemporary biopolitical thought, Hannah Arendt, to help clarify (against her own intentions, as it were) why talk about nonhuman animals *at all* in the context of biopolitics is not simply a category mistake. Arendt brilliantly argues in *The Origins of Totalitarianism* that the idea of "universal human rights" is dubious because it attempts to ground the standing of the subject of rights in the mere biological designation of the human being as *Homo sapiens*, whereas rights themselves are always a product of membership in a political community. They are, as she puts it in *The Human Condition*, "artificial."[20] By contrast, a "human being in general—without a profession, without a citizenship, without an opinion"—belongs "to the human race in much the same way as animals belong to a specific animal species."[21] And more interesting still is Arendt's suggestion that groups founded to support universal human rights and the declarations they frame "showed an uncanny similarity in language and composition to that of societies for the prevention of cruelty to animals."[22]

Arendt is on to something here, but her humanist commitments prevent her from recognizing exactly what it is. Her resistance to what Jacques Derrida will later (and in agreement with Heidegger) reject as "biologistic continuism," and her recourse to what we might call a formal or conventional concept of rights is perfectly correct, as far as it goes, but it is immediately pressured and complicated by the historical fact that the very call of the Universal Declaration of Human Rights of 1948 arose on the basis of the massive presence of stateless persons—persons derived of personhood in precisely her sense—during World War II and its wake. It arose, that is, with the increasingly undeniable presence of what biopolitical thought will canonically come to call "bare life."[23] And so the dilemma she faces is that her formal concept of rights, derived as they are from reciprocal membership in a political community, leaves her no immediately apparent way to recognize the claims of these newly stateless persons whose problem "is not that they are deprived of life, liberty, and the pursuit of happiness," but rather "that they no longer belong to any community whatsoever."[24] But when Arendt confronts the conundrum raised by this historical event—namely, how can the claim of these people be framed, or what constitutes "a right to have rights"?—she falls back on a classically humanist argument that derives from Aristotle: for the "right to have rights" consists in the ability to enter into relations of reciprocal obligation (or what she calls, a little more lyrically, "a framework where one is judged by one's actions and opinions").[25]

Here, then, we find the classic opposition, already familiar to us from Heidegger, of the authentically political as a realm of freedom, choice, "artifice," and so on versus the realm of necessity, utility, and mere "animal" or "natural" existence.[26] And, as in Aristotle, that opposition, like the right to have rights, is grounded in the human being's capacity for speech and language (and a rather naturalistically conceived idea of language at that).[27] As she puts it in *The Human Condition* (virtually paraphrasing Aristotle's famous passage from the *Politics*), "speech is what makes man a political being."[28] Arendt is right to claim—and we will return to these issues in much more detail later—that the designation of those who have standing, who have rights, is a matter of sheer convention outside of any naturalistic ground or biological designation. But she is wrong to claim that the problem raised for humanism by "bare life"—how do we recognize the "right to have rights" for stateless persons but not for "savages" or "beasts" (her terms)[29]—can be solved by the gatekeeper function of speech. Indeed, the most obvious symptom of this conundrum in Arendt's position is that speech appears to be both "natural" *and* "artificial."[30] On the one hand, speech provides the naturalistic basis, specific to humans, of the "right to have rights"; but, on the other hand, speech alone is not enough to secure standing. It has to be "relevant" and recognized, as she puts it—has to hew, that is, to a set of artificial social conventions (indeed, that they *are* artificial and not "natural" is what makes them political).[31]

At this juncture, of course, we might question the relevance of speech for determining the rights-holding subject by means of Jeremy Bentham's famous observation (and Derrida's unpacking of it in *The Animal That Therefore I Am*) that the fundamental question here is not, "can they reason?," or "can they talk?," but "can they suffer?"[32] Here, the issue would be not the paradoxical nature of a speech that is both artificial and natural, redoubled in the difference between "rights" and "the right to have rights" (a right that is, paradoxically, not one), but rather the sheer irrelevance of speech itself to the question of standing (a question we will return to shortly). But what I want to underscore here instead is a logic implicit in Arendt's writings, particularly in *The Origins of Totalitarianism*—a logic that she doesn't quite tease out but one that will be central to biopolitical thought in the decades that follow: the fact, as Esposito puts it, that "the category of those who enjoy a certain right is defined only by contrast with those who, not falling within it, are excluded from it."[33]

And here—to move to the main part of my title—we can begin to glimpse the many senses of what it means to be "before the law": "before" in the sense of that which is ontologically and/or logically antecedent to the law, which exists prior to the moment when the law, in all its contingency and immanence, enacts its originary violence, installs its frame for who's in and who's out. This is the sense of "before" that is marked by Arendt's speculations on the "right to have rights," and it is against such a "before" that the immanence of the law and its exclusions is judged. And thus, "before" in another sense as well, in the sense of standing before the judgment of a law that is inscrutable not just because it establishes by fiat who falls inside and outside the frame, but also because it disavows its own contingency through violence: namely, the violence of sacrifice for which the distinction between human and animal has historically been bedrock, providing for the law the "foundation" for its exclusions that the law cannot provide for itself. As Derrida, Agamben, and others have reminded us, those who fall outside the frame, because they are marked by differences of race, or species, or gender, or religion, or nationality, are always threatened with "a non-criminal putting to death." As Derrida puts it in the interview "Eating Well," "thou shalt not kill" turns out not to be a universalizable maxim, but one that only concerns those for whom it is a "proper" imperative, those who fall inside the frame.[34]

In this light, it is all the more instructive to recall, as Derrida points out in his essay "Before the Law," that when Freud addresses the problem of the origin of law (what is its basis? on what moral foundations does it rest?), he resorts to what amounts to a sacrifice of the animal and, more broadly, of animality, as the means by which both the human and the basis of the law are secured.[35] Here and elsewhere, Freud's concept of "organic repression" marks the point at which the properly human breaks free of and rises above its animal origins, and it is on that basis that moral behavior is founded.[36] But this is not just a "schema of elevation," as Derrida puts it; it is also a "schema of purification"—purification of the animal in "man."[37] Since "man" has to *already* exist to find that which is repugnant in need of repression and thus to rise above it, Freud's search for the origin of law simultaneously marks its own impossibility. Instead, the law is "an absolutely emergent order, absolute and detached from any origin."[38]

But if Derrida is right that this sacrificial structure is fundamental to the entire canonical discourse of "Western metaphysics or religions," the work that it accomplishes is anything but academic, since it is also of "the order of the political, the State, right, or morality," never far from the mundane violence of everyday life.[39] One of the most powerful insights of biopolitical thought is thus to raise this uncomfortable question: if the frame is about rules and laws, about what is proper, and not simply a matter of a line that is given by nature between those inside and those outside, then to live under biopolitics is to live in a situation in which we are all always already (potential) "animals" before the law—not just nonhuman animals according to zoological classification, but any group of living beings that is so framed. Here, the distinction "human/animal"—as the history of slavery, colonialism, and imperialism well shows—is a discursive resource, not a zoological designation; it is, as we will discuss in more detail, a kind of

 dispositif or apparatus. It is all the more ironic, then, that the main line of biopolitical thought has had little or nothing to say about how this logic effects nonhuman beings—a cruel irony indeed, given how "animalization" has been one of its main resources. And it is to that problem that I want to devote my attention in the pages that follow.

II.

In a sense, what follows may be seen as an attempt to explore the extent to which biopolitical thought can help us understand jarring juxtapositions of the sort that I now want to offer in two examples of how nonhuman animals are currently framed at opposite extremes in relation to moral standing and legal protection, how they stand before the law.

First example: On June 25 of 2008, the Environmental Committee of the Spanish Parliament approved resolutions to grant basic rights to Great Apes on a quite traditional model of human rights. To use the language of *The Great Ape Project* coauthored by philosophers Peter Singer and Paola Cavalieri, the three basic rights outlined for this new "community of equals" are 1) "The Right to Life," which means that "members of the community may not be killed except in very strictly defined circumstances" such as self-defense; 2) "The Protection of Individual Liberty," which forbids imprisonment "without due process" and only where it can be shown to be "for their own good, or necessary to protect the public"; and 3) "The Prohibition of Torture," which forbids "the deliberate infliction of severe pain on a member of the community."[1]

Second example: According to statistics provided by the US Department of Agriculture, in the previous year, 2007, about nine billion animals were killed in the United States for food—the vast majority of them raised in Confined Animal Feeding Operations (CAFOs) or "factory farms"—double the number in 1980. This figure does not include the killing of fish, crustaceans, and other farmed animals, nor does it include equines.[2] The National Commission on Industrial Farm Animal Production—a project of the Pew Charitable Trust and the Johns Hopkins Bloomberg School of Public Health—concluded in its final report of 2006 that "at present, federal regulation of the treatment of farm animals is minimal," with the two main pieces of legislation having been passed in 1873 and 1958. With one exception (regarding the slaughter of horses), the commission notes that all other attempts to upgrade federal laws governing standards for farm animal slaughter, housing, and transport have failed—a paucity of regulation that is in marked contrast to federal oversight of many other uses of animals.[3]

I will return to the second example, factory farming, later in these pages, and like the first, it will eventually push us well beyond the purview of current legal doctrine. But it should be noted that even within that limited purview, the commission's assessment is, if anything, overly sanguine. The two primary laws regulating the treatment of nonhuman animals in the United States are the Animal Welfare Act (AWA) and the Humane Methods of Livestock Slaughter Act (HSA). The latter was passed by Congress in 1958, amended in 1978 and 2002, and stipulates that cattle, horses, and other livestock killed for food must be slaughtered with minimal pain and suffering. Before the 1978 amendment, livestock routinely had their throats cut while fully conscious, but now they must, for example, be stunned (or otherwise made insensible) before killing. It is worth noting, however, that 99 percent of the animals killed for food in the United States each year (namely, chickens) are excluded from protection by the HSA—a fact that is doubtless driven by the additional expense that would be incurred by the poultry industry were they to be protected by the law.

The 2002 amendment followed a front-page story in the *Washington Post* in April 2001 called "They Die Piece By Piece" which documented widespread unchecked cruelty in the US slaughterhouse industry.[4] But even after the passage of the 2002 amendment, abuses continue on a massive scale because of one fundamental problem. The law is only as strong as its enforcement, and, as is well documented, the USDA has typically been anything but vigorous in its enforcement of the HSA, as USDA inspectors themselves acknowledge.[5] This fact is less surprising, perhaps, when we remember that the agency itself aids in the marketing and promotion of the very food industries it is charged with regulating.[6] (Indeed, the 2002 amendment in effect simply mandated enforcement of the laws already on the books.) And while it is true that the other main law cited by the commission, the Animal Welfare Act (passed in 1966 and amended several times since), provides more extensive protection, mice, birds, and rats are specifically excluded from the act, and—as with the plight of chickens under the HSA—they make up about 95 percent of all animals used in scientific research in the United States.[7] At the same time, the status of "person" as defined in the AWA includes "any individual, partnership, firm, joint stock company, corporation, association, trust, estate, or other legal entity."[8]

The underlying problem is thus clear. Animals are things and not persons under United States law—things that may or may not have legal status depending on whether or not they have a property relation to an entity designated a "person," who thus has a legal interest in, and standing to argue on behalf of, the animal in question. One obvious solution to this rather counterintuitive state of affairs—and it would be one with wide-ranging economic consequences—would be to eliminate the property status of at least some nonhuman animals by granting them some form of personhood, making them, in turn, potential bearers of rights.[9] But even within existing legal doctrine, we find considerable disagreement about the appropriateness of the "rights" framework for recognizing and protecting the standing of nonhuman animals. On one side, we have legal theorists such as Richard Posner, Cass Sunstein, and Richard Epstein, who believe that the adaptation of the rights model to animals is fundamentally wrong-headed. Epstein, for example, believes that we should continue to treat animals as property, not persons (even in some limited sense), and argues that we should work to minimize harm to animals as long as it does not compromise human gains. He grounds his position in what he regards as a well-justified speciesism. "The root of our discontent," he writes, "is that in the end we have to separate ourselves from (the rest of) nature from which we evolved. Unhappily but insistently, the collective *we* is prepared to do just that. Such is our lot, and perhaps our desire, as human beings."[10] And Posner holds that the most sound approach to the issue is a "humancentric" one that eschews "philosophical argument."[11] "Legal rights," he argues, "have been designed to serve the needs and interests of human beings, having the usual human capacities, and so make a poor fit with the needs and interests of animals."[12]

Now I agree with Epstein about a point I have argued in some detail elsewhere: that animal rights philosophy, in spite of itself, continues to rely on a speciesist (or better, perhaps, anthropocentric) model of subjectivity in its criteria for determining which beings deserve rights.[13] And I think Posner is right that there is "a sad poverty of imagination" in thinking that the issue of animal protection can only be addressed under the rubric of rights.[14] But I would also agree, and more fundamentally, with those at the other end of the animal rights argument—philosophers such as Singer, Cavalieri, and Tom Regan, and legal scholars such as Steven M. Wise and Gary Francione—that positions such as Posner's and Epstein's rely on a thoroughgoing ethnocentrism thinly disguised (and sometimes not disguised at all) as a hard-nosed legal pragmatism giving "straight talk" to the airy philosophers (such as Singer) or those legal scholars overly influenced by them (such as Wise).[15] Posner, for example, wholly subordinates the question of rights to economic utility and political expediency, holding that "legal rights are instruments for securing the liberties that are necessary if a democratic system of government is to provide a workable framework for social order and prosperity. The conventional rights bearers are with minor exceptions actual and potential voters and economic actors. Animals do not fit this description."[16] And Epstein is even more bald in his deployment of what Regan has called the "might makes right" position: "Let it be shown," he asserts, "that the only way to develop an AIDS vaccine that would save thousands of lives is through painful or lethal tests on chimpanzees. . . . An animal right to bodily integrity would stop that movement in its tracks. It will not happen, and it should not happen."[17]

Such positions are question-begging in the extreme, I think, and are easily disposed of, as Singer disposes of Posner's in an exchange that began in the online magazine *Slate*. Singer's criticism makes the same point as Tom Regan's observation that a theory such as Posner's "takes one's moral breath away . . . as if, for example, there would be nothing wrong with apartheid in South Africa if few white South Africans were upset by it."[18] As Singer rightly observes, Posner's legal "pragmatism" is in fact "an undefended and indefensible form of selective moral conservatism."[19] And as for the pragmatics of its "pragmatism," the Posner/Epstein line fares no better. Posner, like Epstein, suggests that the property status of animals is actually a boon to their protection, "because people tend to protect what they own," and like Epstein he suggests that what we mainly need is more vigorous enforcement of laws that prevent "gratuitous cruelty."[20] In a similar vein, Epstein holds that such a position at least "blocks some truly egregious practices without any real human gain, gory lust to one side."[21] But Epstein's contention only gives the lie to Posner's insistence that few of us are "so indifferent to animal suffering, that we are unwilling to incur at least modest costs to prevent cruelty to animals,"[22] for as Singer points out, anticruelty laws do not apply to the case where the largest amount of animal suffering by far takes place—namely, factory farming. Against what Posner calls, without a trace of irony, "the liberating potential of commodification," Singer points out that "we don't have to wonder how many animals suffer and die because they *are* someone's property," because we know that of the nine to ten *billion* animals raised for food in the United States each year, the vast majority—easily several billion—spend their entire short lives in the brutal conditions of the factory farm.[23] Indeed, such anticruelty laws do not even apply to the overwhelming majority of animals used in biomedical research, product testing, and the like, because (as I have already noted) the US Animal Welfare Act of 1966, as amended under the Senate leadership of Jesse Helms in 2002, specifically excludes birds, mice, and rats—that is to say, about 95 percent of the animals used in such research.[24]

As even this brief sketch suggests, one might well conclude that we find an increasingly fraught disjunction between existing legal doctrine and our ability to do justice to nonhuman animals, even as our knowledge of what are taken to be their ethically relevant characteristics and capacities (to suffer, to communicate, to engage in complex forms of social behavior and bonding, and so on) increases dramatically year by year. And more specifically—to stay within the purview of rights discourse a moment more—we find increasing conceptual pressure on the difference between what legal philosophers call "will-based" and "interest-based" theories of rights. The former is rather baldly represented by Posner et al., and the latter grounds the positions of not just Singer and Regan but also of renowned legal philosopher Joel Feinberg, who argues in his influential essay "The Rights of Animals and Future Generations" that it is not enough to say simply that we have (indirect) duties *regarding* animals (the familiar view made famous by Kant[25]); rather, we have (direct) duties *to* (at least some) animals because what is fundamental here is not that they can understand or claim their rights but that—like human infants and mentally impaired people—they are beings who have "conative urges," the "integrated satisfaction of which constitutes their welfare or good" that, as such, deserves protection.[26] Though content to remain within both analytic philosophy and rights discourse, Feinberg's position is related in important ways to attempts to think beyond existing legal frameworks and their philosophical underpinnings in the work of philosophers such as Cora Diamond, Judith Butler, and Jacques Derrida. While Derrida, for his part, is sympathetic with those who protest against the way animals are treated in factory farming, product testing, biomedical experimentation, and the like, he nevertheless believes that "it is preferable not to introduce this problematic concerning the relations between humans and animals into the *existing* juridical framework" by extending some form of human rights to animals.[27] This is so, he argues, because "to confer or to recognize rights for 'animals' is a surreptitious or implicit way of confirming a certain interpretation of the human subject"—an interpretation (and this is demonstrated, it seems to me, in the positions of both Posner and Epstein) that "will have been the lever of the worst violence carried out against nonhuman living beings."[28] So while Derrida is sympathetic with the motivations behind calls for animal rights to protect them from violence, he doesn't support the rights framework per se.[29] And so, Derrida concludes, "For the moment, we ought to limit ourselves to working out the rules of law [*droit*] such as they exist. But it will eventually be necessary to reconsider the history of this law and to understand that although animals cannot be placed under concepts like citizen, consciousness linked with speech, subject, etc., they are not for all that without a 'right.' It's the very concept of right that will have to be 'rethought.'"[30]

A crucial point of emphasis in Derrida's articulation of our ethical responsibility to animals is shared by Cora Diamond, and likewise she finds it actively evaded by the rights model. For Diamond as for Derrida, our shared vulnerability and finitude as embodied beings forms the foundation of our compassion and impulse toward justice for animals—a vulnerability that gets "deflected," as she puts it, by the rights model and the kinds of argument it deploys (pro or con), with its emphasis on agency, reciprocity, and the like. As Diamond puts it,

> The awareness we each have of being a living body, being "alive to the world," carries with it exposure to the bodily sense of vulnerability to death, sheer animal vulnerability, the vulnerability we share with them. This vulnerability is capable of panicking us. To be able to acknowledge it at all, let alone as shared, is wounding; but acknowledging it as shared with other animals, in the presence of what we do to them, is capable not only of panicking one but also of isolating one. . . . Is there any difficulty in seeing why we should not prefer to return to moral debate, in which the livingness and death of animals enter as facts that we treat as relevant in this or that way, not as presences that may unseat our reason?[31]

From this vantage, to try to think about our ethical obligations to animals by deploying the rights model misses the point, not just because the question is thicker and more vexing than the thin if-P-then-Q propositions of a certain style of analytic philosophy but also because "when genuine issues of justice and injustice are framed in terms of rights, they are thereby distorted and trivialized." This is so, Diamond argues, because the rights model, going back to its origins in Roman law, is concerned not with justice and compassion but with "a system of entitlement" and with who gets what within such a system. Instead, she argues, what is crucial to our sense of the injustice done to animals is our repulsion at the brute subjection of the body that they so often endure. For Diamond, the "horror of the conceptualizing of animals as putting nothing in the way of their use as mere stuff" depends on "a comparable horror at human relentlessness and pitilessness in the exercise of power" toward other human beings (in the practice, say, of torturing political prisoners).[32]

To put the question this way is to modulate the discussion of animals, ethics, and law into a different register, one that does not take for granted, much less endorse, our current legal structures for confronting such issues: namely, the register of biopolitics. Here too, the questions of the body and embodiment, and of the political and juridical power over life itself, are fundamental. Take, for example, Judith Butler's *Precarious Life: The Powers of Mourning and Violence*. In the immediate post-9/11 context in which Butler's book was written and to which it responds, the Posner version of legal pragmatism that views the law as that which insures the well-being of "us" and ours over and against "them" takes on much more ominous overtones—particularly in light of the more and more routine suspension of law by executive fiat, the increasingly regularized declaration of a "state of exception" so well analyzed by Agamben and others, that establishes a "no-man's land between public law and political fact, and between the juridical order and life."[33] Against the conjugation of law, power, and community we find in Posner's legal pragmatism, Butler asserts that the fundamental question that needs to be reopened in the current political context is this: "Whose lives count as lives? And finally, What *makes for a grievable life?*" "Is there a way," she asks, "in which the place of the body . . . opens up another kind of normative aspiration within the field of politics," to "consider the demands that are imposed upon us by living in a world of beings who are, by definition, physically dependent on another, physically vulnerable to one another?"[34] "From where," she asks, "might a principle emerge by which we vow to protect others from the kinds of violence we have suffered, if not from an apprehension of a common human vulnerability?"[35]

Yet precisely here, Butler's effort (whose impulses I admire and share, of course) runs aground on the question of nonhuman animals. After all, why should the dangers and vulnerabilities, the exposure to violence and harm that accrue from the fact of embodiment be limited to a "common *human* vulnerability?" Why shouldn't *nonhuman* lives count as "grievable lives," particularly since many millions of people grieve very deeply for their lost animal companions? (I will leave aside for the moment the even more complicated point that at least some nonhuman animals—elephants and great apes, for example—apparently grieve over the loss of those close to them.)[36] Here and there, during the period in which she is working on *Precari-*

ous Life, Butler hints at how her approach to the biopolitical might bear on fundamentally rethinking the human/animal divide. In an interview from 2005, for example, she essentially restates in her own terms Derrida's critique of the fundamentally anthropocentric norms of humanism that require the "abjection" of alterity, whether it be in the form of the "animal," the "inhuman," or the "inorganic."[37] And in an interview from four years later, she suggests that the shared "precariousness" of humans, animals, and the environment "undoes the very conceit of anthropocentrism."[38] Making a distinction that I will develop in much more detail later, Butler is right, I think, to claim in *Frames of War* that "Not everything included under the rubric of 'precarious life'"—plants, for example—warrants protection from harm."[39] And she is also right to criticize "an ontology of individualism" which fails to recognize that the conditions that sustain life are not isolated and limited to "the discrete ontology of the person" but rather imply "the interdependency of persons."[40] But it is not clear, however, why nonhuman animals would not fall under such a definition of "persons" understood as part of a "social ontology" of interdependency since, clearly, some nonhuman animals have their own social relations of interdependency, and still others live in relations of interdependency with human beings—not just in the case of companion animals but also (and in the other direction, as it were) in the case of service animals.[41]

The reasons for this lacuna in Butler's text are complex, I think, and I won't be able to explore them here, but the problem is not, in any event, the perhaps expected one: that animals have an ontologically and existentially different relationship to their finitude than we do, along the lines of Heidegger's existential of "being-toward-death" (which Derrida has convincingly critiqued, to my mind, in connection with the human/animal dichotomy).[42] In fact, Butler is at pains to separate herself from such an ontology in many of her key theoretical and methodological commitments.[43] Rather, the main problems seem to be 1) that Butler's concept of ethics and of community remains tied to a reciprocity model based on a "mutual striving for recognition," and 2) that her notion of subjectivity—and this is a directly related point—remains too committed to the primacy of "agency" for ethical standing, whereas a crucial aspect of taking "embodiment" seriously, if we believe Diamond and Derrida, is that it subverts the overly hasty association of agency with personhood.

As for the first, Butler insists "that each partner in the exchange recognize not only that the other needs and deserves recognition, but also that each, in a different way, is . . . striving for recognition."[44] But what about those members of the community who *aren't* striving for recognition but nevertheless clearly meet the definition of what Butler calls "grievable life"? On the second point, we might linger over Butler's contention that "when we are speaking about the 'subject' we are not always speaking about an individual: we are speaking about a model for agency and intelligibility."[45] And yet her primary examples of vulnerable subjects—newborn infants, for example—have to do (to use the language of analytic philosophy) not with moral agents (those whose *behavior* is subject to moral evaluation) but with moral *patients* (those whose *treatment* is), as in her contention that "primary vulnerability" is a "condition of being laid bare from the start and with which we cannot argue," a "primary scene . . . of abandonment or violence or starvation," of "bodies given over to nothing, or to brutality, or to no sustenance."[46]

To equate standing with moral agents and not moral patients is, of course, a hallmark of the reciprocity model whose most ossified form is Rawlsian contractualism (whose limitations have been convincingly critiqued, to my mind, by Singer, Regan, and Cavalieri, among others).[47] Indeed, as I have argued in some detail elsewhere, I would agree with Derrida, Zygmunt Bauman, and others that the *truly* ethical act is one that is directed toward the moral patient from whom there is no expectation, and perhaps no hope, ever, of reciprocity. Such an act is freely given, outside any model of reciprocity and exchange whose most brazen form is the economic and political template for rights enunciated earlier by Posner.[48] One might think that Butler's invocation of Emmanuel Levinas—whose model of ethics is not one of reciprocity but rather of being held "hostage" to the other in an ethical debt that one can never meet—in the last section of her book might mitigate such a charge. But the problem with Butler's position, as with Levinas's, is its underlying assumption about *who can be* party to an ethical relationship. In Levinas, as we know, such relations concern only those with a "face," and the animal has no face because it has no awareness—no concept, if you like—of its own mortality. But if the embodied vulnerability that subtends all agency "emerges," as Butler puts it, "with life itself," if "we cannot recover the source of this vulnerability" that "precedes the formation of the 'I,'"—that is to say, if our finitude is radical precisely *because* it has no concept—then it is not clear why this does not entail at least some nonhuman as well as human beings.[49]

Butler is certainly right, as many philosophers have emphasized, that "dehumanization" is a fundamental mechanism for producing a "Western" idea of the "man" over and against populations considered "dubiously human."[50] But as I have argued in detail elsewhere, as long as the automatic exclusion of animals from standing remains intact *simply* because of their species, such a dehumanization by means of the discursive mechanism of "animalization" will be readily available for deployment against *whatever* body happens to fall outside the ethnocentric "we." So when Butler calls for "a politics that seeks to recognize the sanctity of life, of all lives," I believe she needs to expand her call across species lines, to declare the human/animal distinction irrelevant, strictly speaking, to such a call. But to do so, she would need to move away from the centrality of reciprocity and agency to ethical and political standing that we find in *Precarious Life*.[51] This is not to offer any specific advice for the moment about "line drawing" with regard to membership in the community (a point I'll return to later); it is simply to suggest that Butler's own theoretical coordinates ought to compel an understanding that the ham-fisted distinction of "human" versus "animal" is of no use in drawing it.

The fundamental conflict in Butler's position is underscored all the more by her focus in *Precarious Life* on the question of Jewish identity and anti-Semitism, simply because that has been Exhibit A in the biopolitical literature of the "animalization" of a population produced as "dubiously human" by and for a political program. I'll return to this traumatic site in some detail in the pages that follow, but to fully understand its many dimensions we need to frame out more fully the background and contours of biopolitical thought as it has evolved from Foucault through the work of Agamben, Esposito, and others. As is well known, Foucault argues in *The History of Sexuality* that "for millennia, man remained what he was for Aristotle: a living animal with the additional capacity for a political existence; modern man is an animal whose politics places his existence as a living being in question."[52] Moreover, as Foucault famously defines biopolitics, it "is the power to make live. Sovereignty took life and let live. And now we have the emergence of a power that I would call the power of regularization, and it, in contrast, consists in making live and letting die."[53] Foucault develops this line of investigation later in his career. In the lectures collected in "*Society Must Be Defended*," for example, he argues that a "new mechanism of power" arose in the seventeenth and eighteenth centuries, one that had "very specific procedures" and "new instruments." This new type of power, he argues, is "absolutely incompatible with relations of sovereignty," and it is based on "a closely meshed grid of material coercions rather than the physical existence of a sovereign."[54]

Foucault thus allows us to see, as Esposito points out, that for biopolitics the fundamental mechanism concerns not sovereignty and law but rather "something that precedes it because it pertains to its 'primary material.'"[55] (As is well known, Foucault's main examples are medicine and the rise of the various "health" professions under the broader regime of "governmentality" and its specifically modern techniques of managing, directing, and enhancing the lives of populations via hygiene, population sciences, food sciences, and so on, the better to extend and consolidate political power.) Even more importantly for our purposes, Foucault argues that this shift from sovereignty to biopower involves a new concept of the subject, one that is endowed with fundamental interests that cannot be limited to or contained by the simple *legal* category of the person. But a trade-off is involved here. If the subject addressed by biopolitics comprises a new political resource, it also requires a new sort of political technology if it is to be fully controlled and exploited. The biosubject, you might say, is far more multidimensional and robust than the "thin" subject of laws and rights; that is both its promise and its challenge as a new object of political power.

As Foucault characterizes it, the subject theorized during this period by English empiricist philosophy is something new, defined not so much by freedom or the struggle of soul versus body but rather as a subject "of individual choices which are both irreducible and non-transferable."[56] Those choices and the ability to make them derive, he argues, not from reason but from the capacity to feel (and the desire to avoid) pain, which is "in itself a reason for the choice beyond which you cannot go." It is a reason beyond reason, you might say, "a sort of irreducible that does not refer to any judgment, reasoning, or calculation."[57] And this means, Foucault argues, that "the subject of right and the subject of interest are not governed by the same logic."[58] (And it is here, as Diamond argues, following the work of Simone Weil, that we may locate the origins of a concept of justice that is not just different from but in fact fundamentally *opposed* to the concept of "rights.")[59]

In opposition to what Foucault calls *homo juridicus* (or *homo legalis*)—the subject of law, rights, and sovereignty—we find in this new subject, *homo oeconomicus*, "an essentially and unconditionally irreducible element against any possible government," a "zone that is definitively inaccessible to any government action," "an atom of freedom."[60] The subject of interest thus "overflows" the subject of right, "surrounds" him and, indeed, is the "permanent condition" of his possibility.[61] *Homo oeconomicus* thus founds a new domain of "irrational rationality" that is of a fundamentally different order from sovereignty and the juridical subject. *Homo oeconomicus* thus says to the sovereign "you cannot because you do not know, and you do not know because you cannot know."[62] But such a creature, of course—and for that very reason—poses a threat to power, one that will in time give rise to the regime of governmentality and its exercise of biopower,[63] which will in turn involve new sciences and discourses: of ratios of birth and death, fertility and mortality rates, figures on longevity—in short, sciences of "populations" whose task it is to manage this aleatory element by "a power that is not individualizing but, if you like, massifying, that is directed not at man-as-body but man-as-species."[64] Foucault thus discloses a key element of the modern political landscape—the "radical transformation of the idea of *humanitas*," as Esposito puts it—that escapes the very political and legal concepts inherited from modernity. "*Humanitas* increasingly comes to adhere to its own biological material,"[65] Esposito writes, and what is involved here is not so much the "animalization" of human populations but rather the exposure of how that designation simultaneously masks and makes possible the more fundamental operations of modern politics by means of what Agamben calls "the anthropological machine, which each time decides upon and recomposes the conflict between man and animal"—a machine that depends on (to use the terms that Agamben borrows from Aristotle) the distinction between *bios* (or political "form of life") and *zoe* (or "bare life").[66]

At this juncture, however, it is worth emphasizing an important difference between Agamben and Foucault—or rather a set of differences whose consequences I want to unfold over the next few pages. While it is no doubt true—both in Foucault's own discourse and in point of fact—that sovereignty continues to be an important force in modern politics, Foucault's point is that it becomes recontextualized, and finally subordinated, to a fundamental political shift. Where Foucault allows us to disarticulate sovereignty and modern biopolitics, Agamben (as Jacques Rancière elegantly puts it) "matches them by equating Foucault's 'control over life' with Carl Schmitt's state of exception."[67] And the result is an overly formalized symmetry between the figure of the sovereign and *homo sacer*, both of whom stand at the extreme opposite limits of a juridico-political order in which they are simultaneously included and excluded, inscribed in the law either by being abandoned by it (in the case of *homo sacer*) or establishing it by extralegal means (in the case of the sovereign). As Agamben puts it, "the sovereign and *homo sacer* present symmetrical figures and have the same structure and are correlative: the sovereign is the one with respect to whom all men are potentially *homines sacri* and *homo sacer* is the one with respect to whom all men act as sovereigns."[68]

Now this exaggerated formal symmetry might seem of little moment—might seem merely academic, you might say—were it not for the fact that it leads Agamben to engage in a fundamental form of dismissal and disavowal of the embodied existence that we share with nonhuman animals—the very existence underscored, as we have seen, by Diamond, Butler, and Derrida.[69] "Agamben remains so fascinated by the hyperbolic opposition between meaningful life and mere animality," Jonathan Elmer argues, "between power and the absolute powerlessness of 'bare life,' that a trace of contempt edges into his description of those who have been reduced to the latter condition"—a fact which expresses itself in any number of odd ways in Agamben's work.[70] For example, as Elmer notes, it leads him to condemn humanitarian aid groups by hewing to a logic that would allow the space between them and the Nazi death camps to become absolutely minimal. As Agamben puts it, humanitarian organizations "can only grasp human life in the figure of bare or sacred life, and therefore, despite themselves, maintain a secret solidarity with the very powers they ought to fight. . . . The 'imploring eyes' of the Rwandan child . . . may well be the most telling contemporary cipher for the bare life that humanitarian organizations, in perfect symmetry with state power, need."[71] The problem, as Rancière notes, is that Agamben subsumes under the same umbrella refugee camps, holding areas for illegal immigrants, the prison at Guantánamo, and much else besides—all of which are in turn assimilated to the fundamental paradigm of the Nazi camps as "the 'nomos' of modernity." And in this highly formalized space, "the executioner and victim . . . appear as two parts of the same 'biopolitical' body," and the polarity of state of exception and bare life "appears as a sort of ontological destiny."[72]

The only alternative to this logic in Agamben's work appears to be what in *The Open* he calls the "suspension of the suspension" of the anthropological machine that ceaselessly reconjugates the relation between the *bios* and *zoe*, human and animal, a radical *Gelassenheit* (or "letting be of Being," to use Heidegger's term).[73] As Agamben writes,

> In our culture man has always been the result of a simultaneous division and articulation of the animal and the human, in which one of the two terms of the operation was also what was at stake in it. To render inoperative the machine that governs our conception of man will therefore mean no longer to seek new—more effective or more authentic—articulations, but rather to show the central emptiness, the hiatus that—within man—separates man and animal, and to risk ourselves in this emptiness: the suspension of the suspension. Shabbat of both animal and man.[74]

What Agamben offers us here, as Dominick LaCapra characterizes it, is a sort of "postsecular negative theology *in extremis*," an "empty utopianism" that should give us pause because of "the linkage among an extremely negative if not nihilistic conception of existing social, political, and cultural reality" and a "desire for re-enchantment of the world."[75]

Agamben's philologically driven formalism thus leads to a remarkable flattening of the differences between different political, ethical, and institutional conjunctures (this, essentially, is Rancière's complaint), a homogenization that is a direct consequence of the severe delimitation of the realm of the "genuinely" political. As a result, as LaCapra notes, attempts to mitigate the legacy of slavery or apartheid, or protests against the genetic manipulation of life or the uneven effects of globalization would not be recognizable as genuine historical or political undertakings.[76] In this light, it is entirely characteristic that in the recent essay "What Is an Apparatus?" Agamben deploys a familiar form of etymological chaining—what Laurent Debreuil has called "philology for show"[77]—to tether Foucault's concept of apparatus, via the root of *dispositif* in *dispositio*, to the "theological legacy" of *oikonomia* and "the redemptive governance of the world and human history" via Providence.[78] And, not surprisingly, that same essay ends with the suggestion that the only authentic political project for "the most docile and cowardly social body that has ever existed in human history" is the "profanation" of contemporary apparatuses (cell phones, mass media, and the like) whose ceaseless work of subjectification and desubjectification are "indifferent" and "do not give rise to the recomposition of a new subject."[79] The essay thus ends on the characteristically apocalyptic note we have been discussing:

> Rather than the proclaimed end of history, we are, in fact witnessing the incessant though aimless motion of this machine, which, in a sort of colossal parody of theological *oikonomia*, has assumed the legacy of the providential governance of the world; yet instead of redeeming our world, this machine (true to the original eschatological vocation of Providence) is leading us to catastrophe. The problem of the profanation of apparatuses—that is to say, the restitution to common use of what has been captured and separated in them—is, for this reason, all the more urgent. But this problem cannot be properly raised as long as those who are concerned with it are unable to intervene in their own processes of subjectification, any more than in their own apparatuses, in order to then bring to light the Ungovernable, which is the beginning and, at the same time, the vanishing point of every politics.[80]

Not surprisingly, such a view of what counts as "genuinely" political in Agamben's work leads to a similar flattening of the category of "the animal" itself, and this in two senses. First, as LaCapra notes, animals in all their diversity "are not figured as complex, differentiated living beings but instead function as an abstracted philosophical topos"[81]—what Derrida calls the "asininity" of the designation "*the* animal." And second—a consequence of the first—Agamben's position provides no means for a politically focused questioning of "the extent to which certain animals, employed in factory farming or experimentation, may be seen in terms of the concept of bare or naked, unprotected life."[82] What gets lost, in other words, is our ability to think a highly differentiated and nuanced biopolitical field, and to understand as well that the exercise of violence on the terrain of biopower is not always, or even often, one of highly symbolic and sacrificial ritual in some timeless political theater, but is often—indeed, maybe usually—an affair of power over and of life that is regularized, routinized, and banalized in the services of a strategic, not symbolic, project.

But if Rancière is right that Agamben's mode of analysis "sweeps aside the heterogeneity of political dissensus" by "infinitizing the wrong, substituting for the processing of a political wrong a sort of ontological destiny," he himself nonetheless shares Agamben's scorn for humanitarian efforts—and not only for NGOs.[83] As Rancière writes,

the age of the "humanitarian" is one of immediate identity between the ordinary example of suffering humanity and the plenitude of the subject of humanity and its rights. The eligible party pure and simple is then none other than the wordless victim, the ultimate figure of the one excluded from the logos, armed only with a voice expressing a monotonous moan, the moan of naked suffering, which saturation has made inaudible. More precisely, the person who is merely human then boils down to the couple of the victim, the pathetic figure to whom such humanity is denied, and the executioner, the monstrous figure of a person who denies humanity.[84]

As Elmer rightly notes, "there is a weird and unsettling version of blaming the victim going on here" in which "the 'merely human' can be understood to have harbored and produced its own contemptuous executioner only by one who shared that contempt."[85] While Rancière's skepticism toward the discourse and mechanisms of "rights" is surely worth heeding, such is the poison fruit, I think, of a dogmatic confidence in the difference between the "genuinely" political and the merely well-intentioned "reformist," as is (a corollary) scorn for an ethics that takes seriously such instances of suffering (regardless of their political context), which then gets rescripted as complicit in the very suffering whose political causes it refuses to address. Or as Rancière puts it, ethics means "the erasure of all legal distinctions and the closure of all political intervals of dissensus."[86] I will leave aside for the moment Rancière's remarkably wooden characterization of ethics as "the infinite conflict of Good and Evil" and simply note that such a pitched posture is shared—to take only two more examples—by both Slavoj Žižek and Alain Badiou, for whom ethics "defines man as a victim." "[T]his 'living being' is in reality contemptible," Badiou writes, "and *he will be held in contempt*. . . . On the side of the victims, the haggard animal exposed on television screens. On the side of the benefactors, conscience and the imperative to intervene. . . . Every intervention in the name of a civilization *requires* contempt for the situation as a whole, including its victims."[87] No doubt Badiou is right, as Elmer notes, to alert us to the hypocrisies of "civilizing" discourses, but the *requirement* of contempt for this "haggard animal" is born from Badiou's own lust for redemption and transcendence, a repudiation of "the 'pathetic figure' of the 'merely human' in favor of a principle of immortality" (or what Badiou calls "the Infinite").[88] Badiou puts it baldly enough: if there is anything such as the "rights of man" they are surely not "rights of survival against misery" but rather "the rights of the Immortal, affirmed in their own right, or the rights of the Infinite, exercised over the contingency of suffering and death."[89]

Žižek, for his own part, finds much to admire in Badiou's posture, and indeed endorses his "*mieux vaut un désastre qu'un désêtre,* so shocking for the liberal sensitivity: better the worse [*sic*] Stalinist terror than the most liberal capitalist democracy." Žižek immediately adds that "of course" when one compares the "positive content" of the two, the latter is "incomparably better," but what is important is "the formal aspect" opened up by the former vis-à-vis "normal" social life.[90] For this reason, Žižek admires the practice employed by the Vietcong (made famous in the film *Apocalypse Now*) of cutting off all of the arms of village children that had been vaccinated by US forces the day before. And he adds, with a truly remarkable lack of irony, "although difficult to sustain as a literal model to follow, this thorough rejection of the Enemy precisely in its helping 'humanitarian' aspect, no matter what the costs, has to be endorsed in its basic intention."[91] "In a similar way," he continues,

> when Sendero Luminoso took over a village, they did not focus on killing the soldiers or policemen stationed there, but more on the UN or U.S. agricultural consultants or health workers trying to help the local peasants. . . . Brutal as this procedure was, it was sustained by the correct insight: they, not the police or army, were the true danger, the enemy at its most perfidious, since they were "lying in the guise of truth"—the more they were "innocent" (they "really" tried to help the peasants), the more they served as a tool of the United States. It is only such a strike against the enemy . . . that displays a true revolutionary autonomy and "sovereignty."[92]

Here, as in Agamben's discussion of the "profanation" of apparatuses, we find the romance of a clean, single line between the space of "genuine" versus merely reformist politics, only here it is the space not of *désoeuvrement* but of an "act" that makes no sense within the existing Symbolic order, an act that is "impossible" and for that very reason "political."[93] And here, as in Agamben and Badiou, Žižek's language is telling. In such a space, "everything is to be endorsed" including "religious 'fanaticism'"; what is wanted is a "leap of faith," the ability to "*step out* of the global circuit."[94] Gestures of "*pure expenditure*," "pure self-destructive ethical insistence, with, apparently, no political goal" are to be endorsed.[95] Though Žižek tries to finesse the point, it is clear that the genuinely political involves the subordination of strategic political interventions to this new space which, defined as it is by its pure *not*-ness in relation to the existing Symbolic structure, partakes of the logic of negative theology. Transcendence or nothing—that is "true" politics.

Now I hasten to add that I agree with Žižek's discussion of "democracy" and his critique of the liberal knee-jerk reaction toward "fanaticism," just as I endorse Rancière's insistence on the importance of the specific conjunctures of political dissensus that get steamrollered by Agamben's ontotheological procedure. But what is fascinating in all these examples is the almost hysterical condemnation and disavowal of embodied life as something constitutively deficient, something that always already has to be redeemed by its radical subordination to a "genuinely political" project for which it is merely the vehicle, merely the gateway to "the immortal" or "the infinite." And so one has to wonder, *pace* Rancière, if the problem here is not with ethics but with *politics* now conceived as the realm of "Good versus Evil." One might pause at this juncture to entertain any number of obvious questions: Are we not witnessing here (as even the most sophomoric psychoanalytic analysis would surely note) a nearly stereotypical disavowal of the fact of our embodied existence that links us fatefully to mortality, and thus to a domain of contingency over which we finally have less than complete control? Is it possible—to stay with that well-worn psychoanalytic motif a bit longer—that we are seeing here the "acting out" of a generation of older (white) (male) (Western) intellectuals who, embittered by the failure during their lifetimes of a "genuinely" "revolutionary" politics, cling ever more desperately to a new sort of "jargon of authenticity" (to use Adorno's phrase), a stark Manichaean opposition of "strong" vs. "weak," "radical" vs. "reformist," "true" vs. "illusory," "inside" vs. "outside," and so on? Do we not indeed find here, as Simon Critchley and others have observed, a tiresome posturing of heroism, machismo, and virility that ought to beg the very kinds of psychoanalytic questions that Žižek himself would be the first to call to our attention (or so one would think)?[96] Is this not indeed a rather familiar type of theology, a "keeping of the faith" in the face of the "televangelization" and suburbanization of religion in the West? In fact, as a number of critics have noted, the rescripting of various religious impulses and imperatives as part of a reclamation of Marxism as an authentic revolutionary moral legacy perhaps should give us pause in an era defined by the Manichaean struggle between Bush's evangelism and Bin Laden's fundamentalism.[97]

III.

Let's return, then, to the question of the body and the political in a lexicon less freighted with the Promethean impulses and transcendental longings characteristic of what Niklas Luhmann would call an "old European" (and, it goes without saying, thoroughgoingly anthropocentric) perspective.[1] Having thus pried apart Agamben and Foucault, we are thus in a better position to emphasize two further dimensions of Foucault's thinking of the biopolitical: one positive or affirmative, and one negative or at least equivocal. The first derives from Foucault's rethinking of the political subject as one who is "before" the law, "underneath" and antecedent to the juridico-political order. What Maurizio Lazzarato calls Foucault's radical "displacement" of the problem of sovereignty doesn't neglect it but merely points out that "the grounding force will not be found on the side of power, since power is 'blind and weak'" (as Foucault puts it) — hence, its growing need, in an increasingly complex and differentiated field of operation, for the various techniques of management, surveillance, and so on that it deploys.[2] What we are dealing with here is not a withdrawal of sovereignty and the law, but rather, as Esposito puts it, how the pivot of real political power gradually shifts from the domain of legal codes and sanctions to "the immanent level of rules and norms that are addressed instead to bodies."[3] Politics, law, and economics now function primarily not in a "top-down" but in "bottom-up" fashion, and become operators for the effective management of the health, well-being, and increase of the population, conceived now as an object of biological intervention. As Jeffrey Nealon characterizes it, "biopower forges an *enabling* link between the seemingly 'universal' categories of population or demography and the 'individual' idiosyncrasies of everyday life. And the proper name for that link is the 'norm.'"[4] "Norms" are thus addressed neither to individual rights holders nor, in Esposito's words, to "their confluence in a people defined as the collective subject of a nation, but rather to the living being in the specificity of its constitution."[5] But that very "specificity," precisely because of its own complexity, which increases all the more as new regimes of knowledge are brought to bear on it, contains new challenges, new "aleatory" elements that must be managed and directed. As Lazzarato argues, three important points follow from this: first, "biopolitics is the form of government taken by a *new dynamic of forces* that, in conjunction, express power relations that the classical world could not have known";[6] second, "the fundamental political problem of modernity is not that of a *single* source of sovereign power, but that of a *multitude of forces*. . . . If power, in keeping with this description, is constituted from below, then we need an ascending analysis of the constitution of power *dispositifs*"; and, third, "Biopower coordinates and targets a power that does not properly belong to it, that comes from the 'outside.' *Biopower is always born of something other than itself.*"[7]

Here, then—with Foucault's emphasis on bodies "before" the law—we find a potentially creative, aleatory element that inheres in the very gambit of biopower, one not wholly subject to the thanatological drift of a biopolitics subordinated to the paradigm of sovereignty. Or, in Nealon's words, in Foucault the power relation names not "a 'negative' relation of domination between *concrete objects, institutions, or persons,* but a 'positive' relation among *virtual forces.*"[8] Indeed, the political payoff of Foucault's analyses of the mechanisms of governmentality resides in no small part in their anatomy of how the machinery of power races to maintain control over the forces it has brought into its orbit—forces that derive in no small part from animal bodies (both human and nonhuman) that are not always already abjected, as they are in Agamben.[9] Quite the contrary, those bodies are enfolded via biopower in struggle and resistance, and because those forces of resistance are thereby produced in specifically articulated forms, through particular *dispositifs,* there is a chance—and this marks in no small part Foucault's debt to Nietzsche (as both Esposito and Deleuze point out)—for life to burst through power's systematic operation in ways that are more and more difficult to anticipate.[10] Power/knowledge complexifies the political resource called the "body," and complexity increases risk. Thus, as Lazzarato notes, Foucault actually "interprets the introduction of 'life into history' constructively because it presents the opportunity to propose a new ontology, one that begins with the body and its potential," over and against the prevailing Western tradition of understanding the political subject as above all a "subject of law."[11] Indeed, Lazzarato argues, one of Foucault's key insights is that without factoring "freedom" and the "resistance of forces" into the equation as constitutive, "the *dispositifs* of modern power remain incomprehensible."[12]

This compels us, then, to firmly distinguish between biopolitics in its declension toward sovereignty as constitutive and biopolitics as a relation of bodies, forces, technologies, and *dispositifs* which, *by definition*, could entail no such formal symmetry between sovereignty and bare life of the sort we find in Agamben (and, as it turns out, in Badiou and Žižek). Consequently, biopolitics is above all a "strategic" arrangement that coordinates power relations "in order to extract a surplus of power from living beings," rather than "the pure and simple capacity to legislate or legitimize sovereignty."[13] And here, what looks like a fairly direct line of descent between Rancière's "dissensus" and Foucault's "resistance" turns out to be, on closer inspection, an important difference. Rancière shares with Foucault the desire to preserve the specificity of the political instance, of articulation and conjuncture (a specificity he finds evacuated in Agamben's ontotheology). But where he differs from Foucault is in his insistence that "a political subject, as I understand it, is a capacity for staging . . . scenes of dissensus."[14] Indeed, Rancière returns to an essentially Aristotelian determination of the political, insisting (classically enough) that "the question of politics begins when the status of the subject able and ready to concern itself with the community becomes an issue."[15] That is to say, Rancière's subject of politics turns out to embody a rather familiar form of intentionality, agency, and reciprocity as constitutive of the political itself. What bears the accent in our analysis of Foucault here, however, is that "resistance" and "freedom" are not to be thought as *constitutively* on the order of "persons" or agents in the traditional sense—not, as Foucault famously put it in his rejection of the term "ideology," of "something on the order of the subject"—but rather of *forces* and *bodies* that only partially coincide with what we used to call the "subject" (indeed, with what we call the "organic"—a point I'll return to in some detail below). As Foucault puts it in an interview from 1977, "power relations can get through to the very depths of bodies, materially, without having been relayed by the representation of subjects. If power affects the body, it is not because it was first internalized in people's consciousness."[16] To put it another way, it is relatively easy to change laws; it is more difficult to change bodies.

Resistance and agency, then, though they may overlap at strategic points, are not by any means coterminous. And we could no more talk about resistance and bodies (including animal bodies) as a matter of agency pure and simple than we could make a similar ascription to children and the forms of child sexuality Foucault studies. For as he puts it in the same interview, "there is a network of bio-power, of somatic-power that is itself a network from which sexuality is born as a historical and cultural phenomenon within which we both recognize and lose ourselves."[17] Rather than remain within the subject/agency vs. object/abjection opposition, then, the power of Foucault's analysis is to demonstrate just how unstable and mobile the lines are between political subject and political object—indeed, to demonstrate how that entire vocabulary must give way to a new, more nuanced reconceptualizaton of political effectivity. And equally important is that Foucault's introduction of "life into history"—of the body in the broadest sense into the political equation—does not lead directly and always already to an abjection for which the most predictable tropes of animalization become the vehicle. For now, it becomes essential, as Lazzarato puts it, "to presuppose the virtual 'freedom' of the forces engaged to understand the exercise of power."[18] This reconceptualization of political subjectivity (if one wants to continue to put it that way) is in no small part what motivates a shift in Foucault's thinking in the 1970s, when he moves from theorizing power on the model of warfare to instead conceptualizing its multivalent and nonlinear nature based on "the potential, difference and autonomy of forces."[19] Foucault's reorientation of the problem has the signal advantage of making the questions of freedom and power questions of degrees and not of kind when it comes to the disposition of human and nonhuman bodies as those are networked with each other and with technologies, practices, and disciplines which may cluster and coconstitute them regardless of species designation.

Take, for example, the use of genetic markers and Estimated Breeding Values (EBVs) in contemporary livestock breeding—a practice which is of a piece with the increasingly pervasive use of genetic knowledges in biosciences generally, as Donna Haraway and Nikolas Rose (among others) have discussed in their very different ways. EBVs constitute a statistical representation of an animal's "genetic merit" based on standardized measurements (an animal's weight at x days old, or the depth or percentage of fat in a particular part of the animal's body, and so on), whereas genetic markers focus on actual genetic locations in the animal's genome that are associated with various traits such as meat tenderness. These are then indexed by private companies that conduct tests on blood and hair samples to establish that a particular animal contains a high level of valuable genetic material, in effect quantifying and linking to genetic markers the value and future performance of the animal and its offspring.[20] As one study notes, such practices "are strongly promoted by state institutions and private companies which claim that they are imperative to modernizing and rationalizing livestock breeding," in contrast to traditional breeding practices such as visual appraisal (or breeding "by eye") and examination of records of breeding ancestry.[21] But such practices have also given rise to resistance in the form of "biosocial collectivities," groups that form (as Rabinow, Rose, and others have argued) in response to emerging scientific discourses of power-knowledge, and often on the basis of shared experience with the blindnesses and oversimplifications of these new regimes (as in, for instance, collectivities formed by patients who share medical experience with a particular condition and its treatment).[22] What is important in the case of EBVs and genetic markers is that these collectivities include nonhuman animals as coconstitutive with human beings in resisting the articulations of a biopolitical *dispositif* in and through the body. Why specifically "bio*political*" and not just "bio*power*"? Because such practices involve not just the insertion of animal bodies into farming assemblages involving technologies, human beings, land, architectural spaces, and so on for the purposes of changing and "maximizing" those bodies, but also the selection of individuals and populations as the bearers of particular traits to suit the particular ends of capitalist enterprise. What we have here, in other words, is not just the operation of a new "norm" but one whose benchmarks presuppose the production and sale of animal food products *as a commodity for profit*.[23] In resistance to this new norm, these new biosocial collectivities assert the importance of care, an intimate understanding of the animal that one might even call "aesthetic," non-"expert" knowledges, and practices of husbandry that do not bear a direct linear relationship to efficiency and profit. For example, many breeders have pointed out that all sorts of factors—some under the control of the breeder, some not—have influences that override genetic composition, and those factors constitute a *complex* of human, animal, and inorganic relations that cannot be wholly anticipated, much less quantified. As one breeder puts it,

> I know damn well that there are an awful lot of influences that are involved in the way a lamb grows and it's not all down to genetics. There's a hell of a lot of external influences there. . . . Because things like prolapses in sheep some of it is genetic, yes, but a lot of it is down to management. If you overfeed those ewes then they are more likely to prolapse. . . . Same with mastitis and growth rates. I know they try to take account of different effects, such as climate and stuff, but even on my farm I've got different land types. I know that some fields are better than others, some might have a terrible time with worms or rain. Sheep do not do well when it's raining all summer, they hate it and don't grow. That is not a genetic effect. It is purely a climate effect and some sheep may fare better than others.[24]

These complex interactions of qualitatively different factors are made manifest in the animal's body, and an experienced, successful breeder's constant adjustment to them is less like statistics and more like choreography, engaging all of the senses and involving both close visual assessment of the animal's comportment (what is often called "the stockman's eye") and deft bodily touch. As one breeder puts it, "you may get these figures as good and then you get there [to a bull sale] and he has a long plain face, which you absolutely hate, and you wouldn't buy that"; another notes, "you have got to handle them, got to handle them and feel the muscle on them and make sure they are structurally sound, good feet and good jaw and everything."[25] In this light, if we take seriously everything that is meant in Foucault's lexicon of biopower by terms such as "bodies," "forces," "resistance" and their aleatory elements—and this is perhaps harder to see in the rhetorical glare of terms like "freedom" and "power"—then we are forced to understand power, freedom, and resistance as modalities of responding to an other who is also taken to be able to respond, but it is a responding that takes place on the basis of forces and capacities that are in no way transparent, or even necessarily accessible to, the subject who responds. In this sense, "resistance comes first" precisely because it resides not just at the level of the body, 'before" the subject who takes thought, but also in the recursive relations of the body with its other—with all its others.

But as Esposito observes—to return to the main line of biopolitical philosophy—all of this leaves us with "a decisive question: if life is stronger than the power that besieges it, if its resistance doesn't allow it to bow to the pressure of power, then how do we account for the outcome obtained in modernity of the mass production of death?" In short, "Why does biopolitics continually threaten to be reversed into thanatopolitics?"[26] Assuming a proximity to Agamben that is greater than I would want to allow—and this is the negative or equivocal aspect of Foucault's thinking of the biopolitical that I mentioned earlier—Esposito argues that Foucault leaves hanging "the question of the relation of modernity with its 'pre,' but also that of the relation with its 'post.' What was twentieth-century totalitarianism with respect to the society that preceded it? Was it a limit, a tear, a surplus in which the mechanism of biopower broke free . . . or, on the contrary, was it society's sole and natural outcome?"[27] Are the Nazi death camps, to use Agamben's words, not "a historical fact and an anomaly belonging to the past," but rather "the hidden matrix and *nomos* of the political space in which we are still living"?[28] If the latter, then Foucault would be forced to join Agamben in seeing genocide as the underlying paradigm and constitutive tendency of modernity.[29] But such a position, as Esposito points out, is at odds not only with Foucault's strong sense of historical distinctions and disjunctions, but also with the sense of life's inevitable expression of itself through resistance that Lazzarato's reading underscores. And so, for Esposito, Foucault's analysis of biopower ends at an impasse, caught between an essentially affirmative view of the biopolitical and a thanatological one.

For Esposito, it is this impasse that the paradigm of "immunization" (one also explored by Derrida, Haraway, and Luhmann, among others) helps us to avoid. In his view, Foucault is unable to develop the full implications of his insight in the lectures of 1976 that "the very fact that you let more die will allow you to live more";[30] he is unable to see that the affirmative and thanatological dimensions of biopolitics—either "a politics *of* life or a politics *over* life," as Esposito puts it[31]—are joined in a single mechanism. "This is where Foucault seeks out the black box of biopolitics," Esposito writes; "in the liminal space where death is not solely the archaic figure against which life defines itself . . . but rather one of its inner folds, a mode—or tonality—of its own preservation."[32] Like Derrida's *pharmakon*, it is "a gentle power that draws death into contact with life and exposes life to the test of death."[33] The immunitary mechanism thus "saves, insures, and preserves the organism, either individual or collective, to which it pertains, but it does not do so directly, immediately, or frontally."[34]

For Esposito, articulating the immunological mechanism with greater precision also allows us to make headway on the question of the specifically modern character of biopolitics. It is certainly the case that the exercise of biopower may be traced to the ancient world—in the availability of slave bodies to their masters, or in the politics of health and hygiene in ancient Rome. But what distinguishes these from modern biopolitics is that such practices were oriented toward a "collective, public, communal" objective.[35] "Tracing it back to its etymological roots," Esposito writes, "*immunitas* is revealed as the negative or lacking [*privata*] form of *communitas*. If *communitas* is that relation, which in binding its members to an obligation of reciprocal donation, jeopardizes individual identity, *immunitas* is the condition of dispensation from such an obligation and therefore the defense against the expropriating features of *communitas*."[36] Such a paradigm can be traced to Hobbes,[37] he argues, in light of whose concept of sovereignty the actual underlying function of what we call "the individual" becomes clear. In reality, it is "the immunitary ideologeme through which modern sovereignty implements the protection of life" — not of the "individual," not even of "the body," but of "life" itself.[38]

Ideologically speaking, the discourse of "the person" or "the individual" doesn't undo the split between the bodily, the "animal" or corporeal on the one hand, and the rational element on the other, but rather serves as a means for the latter to subjugate the former.[39] Here, at the nexus of the "person" or the "individual" and the immunitary mechanism, the biopolitical takes a specifically modern turn, as "the person" becomes the access point, as it were, to life's management and protection. It is with Nietzsche, however, that we find the "irreversible decline of this lexicon," the recognition that such a paradigm is unable to overcome the divisions it establishes between spirit and flesh, right and life, reason and body.[40] With Nietzsche, Esposito argues, the immunitary paradigm achieves its most distinctly modern expression, because "the negative — that which contradicts order, norms, values — is taken on not only as an indispensable element of human history in all its singular or social configurations that it assumes periodically, but indeed as history's productive impulse."[41] In Nietzsche we find "a new horizon of sense" in which "life" is thus suddenly taken to be always already political, the "originary modality" of the politics.[42] As Esposito points out, "If an individual subject of desire and knowledge is withdrawn from and antecedent to the forms of power that structure it; if what we call 'peace' is nothing but the rhetorical representation of relations of force that emerge periodically out of continuous conflict; if rules and laws are nothing other than rituals destined to sanction the domination of one over another," then the anticipation of Foucault's genealogy of biopolitics is already clear.[43]

In this light, Nietzsche's "precocious understanding" is that in the years to come the real political terrain of struggle "will be the one relative to redefining the human species" in relation to its shared borders with both the "animal" and the inorganic (including, of course, the technological).[44] From this vantage, Esposito writes, "in the animalization of man something else is felt that appears to mark more the future of the human species and less the ancestral past . . . [T]he destiny of the animal is enigmatically connected *through* man to him who can exceed him in power and wisdom — to a man who is capable of redefining the meaning of his own species no longer in humanistic or anthropological terms."[45] This makes more sense if we remember, as Vanessa Lemm reminds us in *Nietzsche's Animal Philosophy*, that for him "nature seeks the increasing pluralization of life," and it is on this force that the human must seize in the movement of its own self-realization: "human life cannot bring itself forth by strength alone, but lives entirely out of and against its relation to other forms of life."[46] And this is why, Lemm writes, in contrast to the usual understanding of the *Übermensch* "as the mythic embodiment of the self-sufficient individual," it "is neither an expression of the human as a being independent from the rest of life or from the rest of its own species. Rather, becoming overhuman is dependent upon one's openness to the animality of the human being."[47]

It is this radical dimension of the Nietzschean biopolitical that is amplified in Peter Sloterdijk's famous (or infamous) essay "Regeln für den Menschenpark" ("Rules for the Human Zoo"), where he maximizes the contrast between Nietzsche's "animal philosophy" and Heidegger's "antivitalistic passion," his insistence that man is not just "an animal with a cultural or metaphysical addition."[48] What Heidegger's humanism doesn't grasp is that "man is the shepherd of being" (to use Heidegger's famous phrase) in a far more literal and fraught sense, one that will eventually be realized by the contemporary realities of eugenics, bioengineering, and the selective manipulation of life at the most elementary level. Sloterdijk writes,

> The humanist directs himself to the human, and applies to him his taming, training, educational tools, convinced, as he is, of the necessary connection between reading, sitting, and taming.
>
> Nietzsche . . . thought to see behind the horizon of scholarly man-taming a second, darker horizon. He perceived a space in which the unavoidable battle over the direction of man-breeding would begin. . . .
>
> This is the root of the basic conflict Nietzsche postulates for the future: the battle between those who wish to breed for minimization and those who wish to breed for maximization of human function, or as we might say, a battle between humanists and superhumanists.[49]

While "petty politics" for Nietzsche concerns regulating the field of the normal and the everyday, what he calls "great politics" involves "not only a different distribution of power, and not even the choice of the best regime or the best political party, but rather, and foremost the definition of what human life is today and what it may become tomorrow."[50] But it also, and more menacingly, concerns a process of selection and screening bent toward extinguishing the "weak."[51] The "strong" or "firm" type and the "weak" or "fatigue" type are locked in a never-ending struggle as two sides of that same being called "human," and the "herd" needs a shepherd to actualize it as a political medium.[52] As Sloterdijk observes, "it may well be that Zarathustra was the spokesman of a philosophical hysteria whose infectious effect is today, and perhaps forever, banished. But the discourse about difference and the control of taming and breeding—indeed, just the suggestion about the decline of awareness of how human beings are produced, and intimations of anthropotechnology—these are prospects from which we may not, in the present day, avert our eyes."[53] From this Nietzschean vantage, the cardinal biopolitical sin of contemporary practices such as factory farming, or subjecting "purpose-bred" animals to routinized experimentation in which they are little more than conduits for statistical throughput, is not just the pain and suffering it causes (these, for Nietzsche, would not be paramount) but rather the deadening and diminishing of "animality" itself in all its vitality, creativity, and multiplicity, which would in turn forestall our own ability to discover the multiplicity in ourselves via animality as a creative force for our own evolution. In the docility and torpor of the factory farm, where the ratio of purpose-bred harvestable flesh to resistance is calculated to be as high as possible, Nietzsche and Sloterdijk would suggest that we humans catch a glimpse of our own biopolitical future, the "herd" toward which the masses of humanity are inexorably tending.

In Nietzsche's emphasis on "the vital impulse" of animality as a creative, aleatory force, we find an obvious point of contact with Derrida's understanding of the "multiplicity" of nonhuman life that motivates his rejection of the phrase "*the* animal," and with Deleuze and Guattari's sense of "becoming-animal" in *A Thousand Plateaus*.[54] But the fundamental difference between these and Nietzsche is the latter's "immunological" casting of the relations of the "weak" and the "strong," marked as it is by assertions such as the following: "the crucial thing about a good and healthy aristocracy, however, is that it . . . has no misgivings in condoning the sacrifice of a vast number of people who must *for its sake* be oppressed and diminished into incomplete people, slaves, tools."[55] And in this, Esposito rightly notes, Nietzsche's position can be seen as "an atrocious link in the gallery of horrors" that stretches from the eugenics and selective breeding of Nietzsche's own century to the Nazi death camps in the century that would follow.[56]

IV.

We are returned, then, not just to the thanatopolitical site of the camps that takes center stage in Agamben's work, and not just to the question of the biopolitical status of Nazism, but also to the central function of race—and by extension, species—in modern biopolitics. As is well known, Foucault explores this topic in the lectures from 1975–76 collected in *"Society Must Be Defended."* Racism, as Foucault notes, creates "caesuras within the biological continuum addressed by biopower"; it is "a way of fragmenting the field of the biological that power controls" so that some populations may be killed or allowed to die—what Foucault bluntly calls "indirect murder."[1] "In a normalizing society," he writes, "race or racism is the precondition that makes killing acceptable."[2] And it has a second function, he argues: "the death of the bad race, of the inferior race (or the degenerate, the abnormal) is something that will make life in general healthier: healthier and purer."[3]

As we have seen, Esposito's immunitary paradigm seizes on and develops this realization by Foucault, but the point I want to emphasize here is Foucault's recognition that you can't talk about biopolitics without talking about race, and you can't talk about race without talking about species, simply because both categories—as history well shows—are so notoriously pliable and unstable, constantly bleeding into and out of each other. Exhibit A here, of course, is the analogy between humans and animals that characterizes much of the literature on the Holocaust. As is well known, the word means "burnt offering" and was taken from the Greek word *holokauston*, which referred to the ancient practice of sacrificing animals.[4] And even better known, perhaps, is the common refrain of those subjected to the violence of the camps: "we were treated like animals."[5] But as Esposito's bracing analysis of Nazi genocide shows, the mainspring of this process cannot exactly be said to be the "animalization" pure and simple of the Jews and other victims:

> More than "bestializing" man, as is commonly thought, [Nazism] "anthropologized' the animal, enlarging the definition of *anthropos* to the point where it also comprised animals of inferior species. He who was the object of persecution and extreme violence wasn't simply an animal (which was indeed respected and protected as such by one of the most advanced pieces of legislation of the entire world), but was an *animal-man*. . . . [T]he regime promulgated a circular that prohibited any kind of cruelty to animals, in particular with reference to cold, to heat, and to the inoculation of pathogenic germs. Considering the zeal with which the Nazis respected their own laws, this means that if those interned in the extermination camps had been considered to be *only* animals, they would have been saved.[6]

While Esposito overstates his case here (as Singer points out, following Boria Sax's extensive work on the topic, the Nazis routinely conducted painful and even brutal experiments on animals such as primates[7]), his analysis does have the virtue of complicating our understanding of the relationship between the human/animal distinction and the *bios/zoe* doublet of biopolitics (a point I'll return to in more detail below). And with this more complicated conceptual topography in mind, we can revisit the "animal Holocaust" analogy that has been widely used to describe our treatment of animals in factory farming and biomedical testing.

Jacques Derrida is particularly forceful on this point in his later work, where he pulls no punches in criticizing "this violence that some would compare to the worst cases of genocide," a genocide made even more perverse by the fact that millions of animals are "exterminated *by means of their continued existence or even their overpopulation.*" Derrida (an Algerian Jew) is well aware of the complexities of the analogy here, of course, and he reminds us that "one should neither abuse the figure of genocide nor too quickly consider it explained away."[8] Indeed, his ending observation— "*by means of their continued existence*" —points us toward some important differences between the two cases that Esposito will explore as well. For example, in the Nazi camps, we find those who *had been* citizens, members of the community, now stripped of every legal protection and right by means of the declaration of a "state of exception," whereas in the factory farm, we find those who *never were* members of the community nevertheless afforded at least some minimal protection (humane slaughter laws, for example), even if those laws are in fact minimally enforced.[9] Similarly, the "animal Holocaust" of factory farming does not abide by the logic of genocide per se, since the minimal conditions of genocide agreed on by most scholars are that a sovereign state declares an intention to kill a particular homogeneous group not for economic or political reasons but rather because of that group's biological constitution, and that such a project of killing will be potentially complete, resulting in the extermination of all members of the targeted group.[10] Indeed, this is part of what makes the "animal Holocaust" not just horrible but in an important sense perverse—what Derrida calls a "virtually interminable survival, in conditions that previous generations would have judged monstrous, outside of every presumed norm of a life proper to animals."[11] And this "interminable survival" leads, in turn, to a massive difference in sheer scale between the two cases, as nearly ten *billion* animals are raised for food each year in the United States, the vast majority of them in factory farms. In fact, nine hundred million of these animals each year never even make it to the slaughterhouse for their merciful end, because they die first of stress, disease, or injury.[12]

At the same time, it hardly needs pointing out that the practices of modern biopolitics have forged themselves in the common subjection and management of both human and animal bodies—a fact brought very sharply into focus in scholarship that examines the analogies between the technological manipulation of life in the factory farm and in the Nazi camps. As one writer notes, "the methods of the Holocaust exist today in the form of factory farming where billions of innocent, feeling beings are taken from their families, trucked hundreds of miles through all weather extremes, confined in cramped, filthy conditions and herded to their deaths."[13] As another points out, "American eugenics and assembly-line slaughter crossed the Atlantic Ocean and found fertile ground in Nazi Germany."[14] In fact, the assembly line processes used to kill Jews in Nazi Germany derived from production models originally developed by Henry Ford (a notorious anti-Semite), who in turn reveals in his autobiography that the inspiration for his assembly-line method came from a visit to a Chicago slaughterhouse where he witnessed its mechanized *disassembly* line for making meat out of animal carcasses.[15]

From the vantage of a Foucauldian biopolitics, then, we are forced to conclude that current practices of factory farming and the like—while crucially different from the logic of the Holocaust and of genocide in the ways I have just noted—constitute not just some embarrassing sideline of modern life that has nothing to do with politics proper, and which can be well regulated by an adjacent set of anticruelty laws that do not intersect with politics as such in any fundamental way. Rather, such practices must be seen not just as political but as in fact *constitutively* political for biopolitics in its modern form. Indeed, the practices of maximizing control over life and death, of "making live," in Foucault's words, through eugenics, artificial insemination and selective breeding, pharmaceutical enhancement, inoculation, and the like are on display in the modern factory farm as perhaps nowhere else in biopolitical history. It can hardly be debated, I think, that "the animal" is, today—and on a scale unprecedented in human history—the site of the very ur-form of that *dispositif* and the face of its most unchecked, nightmarish effects.

Insofar as the biopolitical per se is tethered to the question of sovereignty as its constitutive term, the treatment of animals in factory farming, product testing, and so on, could not be deemed properly "political" at all. And an appeal for something like "animal rights" would, from a Schmittian point of view, fare no better than an appeal for "human rights" that exceeds or comes "before" the claims of the sovereign nation-state. Indeed, as Derrida summarizes it in *The Beast and the Sovereign*, from Schmitt's point of view, wherever calls for universal human rights that exceed the contingent rights of the citizen are made, whenever one invokes the idea of "crimes against humanity" to implement a universal or international right, the authority and sovereignty of the nation-state is called into question—and always, in fact, by another sovereignty.[16] Such a call is, Schmitt argues in *The Concept of the Political*, a "de-politicizing" predication, an "an ideological disguise," as Derrida puts it. And so "humanity is only a word, then, a name in the name of which particular and momentary interests of particular states are served."[17]

We have already touched on some of the problems with this concept of the political in our discussion of Arendt at the outset of this essay, but a different sort of challenge to the sovereignty/decisionist line that runs from Schmitt to Agamben is posed, as Penelope Deutscher notes, by the problem of abortion and fetal "life"—a topic about which Agamben, as she points out, is almost entirely silent.[18] As we have already seen, Agamben draws our attention to the "beyond" or the "before" of the human in the form of the *bios/zoe* difference. But what if we ask, with Andrew Norris, what we do when we confront the question of those entities that have not already been recognized as rights bearers.[19] From Deutscher's perspective, the fetus is neither *zoe* nor *bios*, but in public clashes over abortion it is "rhetorically and varyingly depicted as all of these," so that it is often erroneously represented in antiabortion contexts as "as a form of politicized bare life exposed to sovereign violence"—namely the violence of the woman considering an abortion who may be "figured as a potentially murderous competing sovereign whose self-interest would thwart the intervening motivations of the state concerned with the threshold life in question."[20] From this vantage, she argues, "Agamben's work might appear one step closer to an interested reading by the antiabortion activist whose extremism has extended to the passion for comparisons with Auschwitz."[21] At which point, she rightly suggests, we realize some of the dangers attendant on the radical formal symmetry of sovereign and bare life in Agamben's work, and we would do well instead to pay attention, say, to "the interconnections between biopower and women's reproductivity," and the overdeterminations of both in the history of abortion regulation.[22] We would do well, that is, to recalibrate our understanding of the biopolitical in terms of the *dispositifs* of biopower and their political articulation rather than the metaphysics of sovereignty.

The same holds for "the animal," of course, which is, if anything, even *more* differentially and heterogeneously situated, depending on its status as factory farm commodity, companion animal, wildlife, or much else besides. The "fetus that is falsely figured as *homo sacer*" is literally *nothing like* the fully formed creatures whose physiological plasticity registers, remembers, and responds to the history of what has befallen it in the form of hopes, expectations, fears—a point I'll come back to momentarily.[23] What all of this suggests is that the accent we find in Lazzarato's reading of Foucault makes sense—and with it, that we need to differentiate more than Esposito would between Foucault and Agamben, drawing out how a reading of biopolitics that focuses on *dispositifs* rather than sovereignty enables us to think a much more complex and highly differentiated biopolitical field. What is needed, then, is another *thought* of the biopolitical in which human and nonhuman lives are deeply woven together de facto even if, de jure, they "politically" have nothing to do with each other (and how could they, if animals are "things" and humans are "persons"?).

For example, a recent study by the Pew Commission on Industrial Farm Animal Production points out that factory farming may seem good at producing edible animal products at the lowest possible cost, but "there is evidence," as the *New York Times* puts it, "that this model is economically viable only because it passes on health costs to the public—in the form of occasional salmonella, anti-biotic resistant diseases, polluted waters, food poisoning and possibly certain cancers."[24] A nearly one-hundred-page report done in 2008 by the Union of Concerned Scientists lists in excruciating detail the costs—both direct and indirect—borne by society for the mass-produced, industrialized killing of animals for food. Between 1997 and 2005, US taxpayers handed over to CAFOs roughly 3.8 billion dollars a year in the form of "indirect" subsidies—chiefly in the form of government handouts to growers of corn and soybeans, the majority of which is eaten by livestock animals each year. Such subsidies artificially reduce the price of meat, poultry, and pork, and other direct subsidies further artificially reduce the costs of factory farming by shifting costs to the taxpayer. Chief among these is the Environmental Quality Incentives Program, which gives CAFOs about 100 million dollars per year, in effect forcing taxpayers to help pay the environmental cleanup costs for factory farms. Added to these are the massive but more difficult to quantify "external" costs of CAFOs, which include environmental degradation and pollution of air and water that result from the large amount of energy use and animal waste generated by CAFOs, reduced quality of life for rural communities (including lower property values), and so on. To even modestly reduce the water and air pollution they create would cost CAFOs more than $1 billion per year, and other external costs would likely run into the billions.[25]

Given the "immunitary" paradigm we have been discussing, one of these external costs—those associated with the use of antibiotics in factory farms—is worth dwelling on for a moment. As a recent *New York Times* article reports, 80 percent of the antibiotics used in the United States go to livestock on factory farms—nearly all of it administered in their food and water—and typically to healthy animals to prevent them from becoming sick from the cramped and squalid conditions they endure. In fact, the single state of North Carolina uses more antibiotics for its livestock than the entire country uses for its human population. Not surprisingly, this has led to a startling increase in antibiotic-resistant pathogens—chief among them, MRSA, an antibiotic-resistant staphylococcus bacterium that annually kills more people than AIDS. It was recently found in 70 percent of hogs on one factory farm, and in 45 percent of employees at another.[26] When such pathogens, born of our own maltreatment of farm animals, pose a risk to national biosecurity, the results are depressingly familiar and send us back to our earlier discussion of "animal Holocaust": in England, millions of pigs, cows, and sheep shot and bulldozed into graves and burned during the foot-and-mouth disease epidemic of 2001; in California, the killing of nine million hens to thwart Newcastle disease in the 1970s; and millions of chickens, turkeys, and ducks killed worldwide—80 million alone in Southeast Asia, 19 million more in Canada—to combat H5N1 avian influenza in the spring of 2004.[27]

The fundamental biopolitical logic identified by Foucault and developed by Esposito is unmistakable here. As Foucault writes in his analysis of medicalization, the harmful effects of medication are "due not to errors of diagnosis or the accidental ingestion of those substances, but to the action of medical practice itself . . . precisely because of their efficacy," leading humankind "into a perilous area of history."[28] As Esposito notes, "as in all areas of contemporary social systems, neurotically haunted by a continuously growing need for security, this means that the risk from which the protection is meant to defend is actually created by the protection itself"—a logic that is, as we have seen, "inscribed at the heart of modern biopolitics."[29]

What we need to remember here is that biopolitics acts fundamentally not on the "person" or the "individual," nor even, finally, on "the body," but rather at the even more elemental level called "flesh," which is "nothing but the unitary weave of the difference between bodies. It is the non-belonging, or rather the intra-belonging," Esposito writes, "which allows what is different to not hermetically seal itself up within itself, but rather, to remain in contact with its outside."[30] To put it in systems theory terms, we might say that "the body" obtains at the level of autopoietic "organization" and its closure, while "the flesh" obtains at the level of "structure," opening the autopoietic unity to the flows of energy and organic material that both sustain it and potentially threaten it.[31] Flesh "is neither another body nor the body's other: it is simply the way of being in common of that which seeks to be immune," for which the distinction between "human" and "animal" is no longer an adequate lexicon, as even Nietzsche realized.[32] "Flesh" thus becomes the communal substrate shared by humans with other forms of life in and through which "the body" is both sustained and threatened, and the more we attempt to maximize the former through the micrological manipulations of biopower, the more the threat increases. So when we consider the use of CAFOs to feed the majority of the population—their effects on public health (and therefore on public health policy and its escalating costs), their devastating, literally unsustainable effects on the environment, and the use of massive government subsidies to prop up the entire system—is it really possible to isolate all of these from the political per se? And if so, is it not a thin and impoverished understanding of "the political" that is the result?

As Foucault puts it in an interview from 1977,

The political is not what ultimately determines (or overdetermines) elementary relations. . . . All relations of force imply a power relation . . . and each power relation can be referred to the political sphere of which it is a part, both as its effect and as its condition of possibility. . . . Political analysis and critique, for the most part, have to be invented—but so do strategies that will allow both modifying these relations of force and coordinating them in such a way that this modification will be possible and register in reality. That is to say that the problem is not really defining a political "position" (which brings us back to a choice on a chessboard that is already set up), but to imagine and to bring out new schemas of politicization.[33]

Indeed, over and against the predictable Manichaean idea of the political that announces itself in Badiou, Žižek, et al., we find here a fundamental rethinking of political effectivity itself, one that is not simply a site of an ontological repetition compulsion, one that does not simply take for granted traditional notions of the political "agent" or "subject" counterpoised over and against the world or "objects," but is rather addressed precisely to the new conceptualization of politicization opened up by biopolitics—to those (that is to say, *all* of us) who are caught up in the play of biopower, whose status as "subjects" or as "objects" is floating, indeterminate, and always subject to strategic rescripting.

From this vantage, opposing factory farming would constitute a "new schema of politicization," not just in resisting the formative *dispositifs* of modern biopolitics in their most brazen form, but also in articulating with other dimensions of political resistance, such as opposition to the commodification and private ownership of life in the services of late capitalism. In this light, paying attention to the question of nonhuman animal life has the potential to actually radicalize biopolitical thought beyond its usual parameters. As Nicole Shukin points out, the problem with biopolitical thought, from whatever location on the political compass, has been twofold. First, time and again it "bumps up against its own internal limit at the species line"; and second, biopolitical analyses have been "constrained by their reluctance to pursue power's effects beyond the production of human social and/or species life and into the zoopolitics of animal capital."[34] This is patently true in both the tacitly liberal democratic orientation of Nikolas Rose in *The Politics of Life Itself* and in the sort of post-Marxist work that would oppose it, such as Paolo Virno's *A Grammar of the Multitude*.[35] As Shukin's study makes abundantly clear, the question of the animal that biopolitics has ignored is not just conceptual or analytical but *material*, involving not just "the semiotic currency of animal signs" but also "the carnal traffic in animal substances."[36] As she puts it, the private ownership and manipulation of animal bodies, where they "are reproductively managed as protein and gene breeders under chilling conditions of control," are crucial to the flows of speculation and investment in biocapitalism that Rose describes but doesn't quite critique.[37] Moreover, as phenomena such as "mad cow disease" and "avian flu" make clear, the "formerly distinct barriers separating humans and other species are imaginatively, and physically, disintegrating under current conditions of globalization."[38]

Taking such questions seriously poses rather direct *political* challenges and radicalizes biopolitical thought in ways not possible if we remain within the usual purview of anthropocentrism. Think, for example, about the immediate practical consequences of eliminating the legal designation of animals as property. As Matthew Calarco puts it,

> On this political terrain, neohumanist arguments concerning the merits of the democratic tradition have little if any weight. Even if one were to inscribe animal rights within a democratic liberatory narrative of expansion and perfectibility (as is sometimes done), such gestures can only appear tragicomic in light of the massive institutionalized abuse of animals that contemporary democracies not only tolerate but encourage on a daily basis.[39]

One thing seems clear: Such practices are part of a matrix that, under conditions of globalization, increasingly takes as its political object planetary life itself, at the level of "flesh," and they constitute a biopolitics that encompasses and conjoins the putatively opposed political regimes of liberal democracy, fascism, and communism. They involve the exponential expansion and routinization of mechanisms and logics that extend from the Chicago slaughterhouses of the turn of the twentieth century, through the assembly lines developed by Ford, to the Nazi death camps and back again, traversing what we are now forced to call a newly expanded community of the living.

V.

Here, however, in the face of this massive thanatological drift of modern biopolitics, we need to remember the fundamental ambivalence of Foucault's notion of biopower, an ambivalence underscored, as we saw earlier, by both Lazzarato and Nealon. For at the very historical moment when the scale and efficiency of factory farming has never been more nightmarish, in which the oceans are being overfished by advanced techniques such as purse-seine netting to the point of collapse,[1] some animals are receiving unprecedented levels of care, so much so that the pet care industry in the United States grew in total expenditures from $17 billion in 1994 to nearly $36 billion in 2005 and to $45.5 billion in 2009.[2] The late 1990s saw the birth of the famous Missyplicity Project, dedicated to cloning companion animals for those who can afford it, and, short of that (as any owner of a companion animal will testify), the range and quality of veterinary care available today, much of it highly specialized and expensive (dental cleaning requiring general anesthesia, ultrasounds, CAT scans, EKGs, chemotherapy for veterinary oncology, and much else besides—the capacity to "make live," in Foucault's words), far outstrips what was either available or marketable even a generation ago.[3] And this has led in turn to another growth industry unheard of until relatively recently: pet health care insurance, currently estimated to be a $271 million business on track to balloon to $500 million in 2012.[4] What all this adds up to, of course, is a historically remarkable shrinkage in the gap between human beings and their animal companions regarding quality of life in areas such as food, health care, and other goods and services.[5]

At the nether end of these developments, we find examples such as the rapidly expanding field of pet pharmacology. Critics like to describe it—and the booming pet services industry generally—as essentially yet another lifestyle foible of the well-to-do, especially baby boomers who no longer have dependent children and thus enjoy increased affluence.[6] Here as elsewhere (so the story goes), what the public wants is a pill to take care of the problem and do the work. As one staunch opponent of treating companion animals' behavioral problems with drugs observes, "what people want is a pet that is on par with a TiVo, that its activity, play and affection are on demand. . . . Then, when they're done, they want to turn it off."[7] But it's not quite as simple as that, either ontologically or biopolitically. For as one writer notes, the increasing use of "modern pet pharma" may seem silly—the drug Reconcile given to dogs to treat separation anxiety is exactly like Prozac, for example, only it's chewable and tastes like meat—but it raises questions such as the following: "If the strict Cartesian view were true—that animals are essentially flesh-and-blood automatons, lacking anything resembling human emotion, memory and consciousness—then why do animals develop mental illnesses that eerily resemble human ones and that respond to the same medications?"[8] And as for the biopolitical dimension, some veterinary behavioral pharmacologists have pointed out that because Prozac, Paxil, and other drugs were tested for efficacy in laboratory animals long before they were prescribed to humans, "You can plausibly argue . . . that humans are in fact using animal drugs" and not the other way around.[9] Clearly, then, many animals flourish not in spite of the fact that they are "animals" but *because* they are "animals"—or even more precisely, perhaps, because they are felt to be members of our families and our communities, regardless of their species. And yet, at the very same moment, billions of animals in factory farms, many of whom are very near to or indeed exceed cats and dogs and other companion animals in the capacities we take to be relevant to standing (the ability to experience pain and suffering, anticipatory dread, emotional bonds and complex social interactions, and so on), have as horrible a life as one could imagine, also *because* they are "animals." Clearly, then, the question here is not simply of the "animal" as the abjected other of the "human" *tout court*, but rather something like a distinction between *bios* and *zoe* that obtains within the domain of domesticated animals itself.

We find here an additional insight that thickens Derrida's well-known observation that the designation "*the* animal" is an "asininity" because it effaces the vast diversity of nonhuman life under a single definite article. Indeed, we might say, paraphrasing Esposito, that "*the* animal" is an "ideologeme" that masks what Rosi Braidotti, following Deleuze, calls the "transversal" relations in which animals, and our relations with them, are caught under biopolitical life.[10] From this vantage, it makes little or no sense to lump together in the same category the chimpanzee who endures biomedical research, the dog who lives in your home and receives chemotherapy, and the pig who languishes in the factory farm. Nor does it even make sense to assume that such groupings proceed along species lines, strictly speaking. As Braidotti puts it, "In the universe that I inhabit as a post-industrial subject of so-called advanced capitalism, there is more familiarity, i.e. more to share in the way of embodied and embedded locations, between female humans and the cloned sheep Dolly, or oncomouse and other genetically engineered members of the former animal kingdom, than with humanistic ideals of the uniqueness of my species."[11]

This new differentiation of the biopolitical field is what Esposito is after at the end of *Bios*, where he insists that a turn away from the thanatological and autoimmunitary logic of biopolitics can only take place if life as such—not just human (vs. animal) life, not just Aryan (vs. Jewish) life, not just Christian (vs. Islamic) life—becomes the subject of immunitary protection. Esposito writes,

> We can say that the subject, be it a subject of knowledge, will, or action as modern philosophy commonly understands it, is never separated from the living roots from which it originates in the form of a splitting between the somatic and psychic levels in which the first is never decided [*risolve*] in favor of the second. . . . This means that between man and animal—but also, in a sense, between the animal and the vegetal and between the vegetal and the natural object—the transition is rather more fluid than was imagined.[12]

And what this means, in turn, is that "there is a modality of *bios* that cannot be inscribed within the borders of the conscious subject, and therefore is not attributable to the form of the individual or of the person."[13] To put it another way, if Agamben's contribution is to articulate powerfully how the "anthropological machine" *cannot function* without producing this remainder called "animal," which is at the same time the retroactively posited origin that must be excluded by the political project of "man," then Esposito's advance is not just to recognize the centrality of race in biopolitics but to strike a powerful blow against it by suggesting that "the animal" is not something that need be always already abjected. But if one of the great contributions of biopolitical thought is to show how it is impossible to talk about race without talking about species (and vice versa), what must now be added (and it is already at work in Derrida's critique of the idea of "*the* animal" in the singular) is that race and species must, in turn, give way to their own deconstruction in favor of a more highly differentiated thinking of life in relation to biopower, if the immunitary is not to turn more or less automatically into the autoimmunitary. Or in Esposito's words, "the most complete normative model is indeed what already prefigures the movement of its own deconstruction in favor of another that follows from it," a movement driven by the fact that "there is never a moment in which the individual can be enclosed in himself or be blocked in a closed system, and so removed from the movement that binds him to his own biological matrix."[14] The strength of Esposito's position is that it demands that we think the norm and the form of life together in one movement, and that we do so cognizant of the fact that what we used to call the "subject" of the norm and its "living roots" are always already embedded in what we might call a "hyphenated" relationship (to use Gregory Bateson's formulation): not organism over and against its environment, but organism *in* its environment.[15]

But where Esposito is wrong, I think, is in his insistence on "the principle of unlimited equivalence for every single form of life."[16] The problem, of course (or one of the problems), is that if all forms of life are taken to be equal, then it can only be because they, as "the living," all equally embody and express a positive, substantive principle of "Life" not contained in any one of them. Thus, as Eugene Thacker puts it, "the contradiction is clear: Life is that which renders intelligible the living, but which in itself cannot be thought, has no existence, is not itself living."[17] As Thacker points out, later philosophers such as Kant "would recast this dilemma in terms of an antinomy: every assertion about life as inherently ordered, organized, or purposeful is always undermined by the assertion itself and its irrevocable object of thought."[18] But, of course, such a Kantian solution is precisely what is unavailable to Esposito, given his reliance on Simondon and Deleuze in the final pages of *Bios* and its framing of an affirmative biopolitics.

To put this slightly otherwise—updating the Kantian position via Derrida—what Esposito is unable to articulate is that what "binds him to his own biological matrix" is nothing "living," but neither is it "Life." Rather, as Martin Hägglund has argued, it is the trace-structure and "spacing" that is "the condition for anything that is subject to succession, whether animate or inanimate, ideal or material."[19] Such a structure (or more precisely, system) is, strictly speaking "dead"; it is a "*machinalité*" (to use Derrida's term).[20] Far from metaphysical, however, such a system is perfectly compatible with a materialist and naturalistic account of how life evolves out of nonliving matter, how even the most sophisticated forms of intentionality or sensibility arise out of the inorganic systematicity of repetition and recursivity, retention and protention.[21] What Henry Staten calls the "strong naturalist view" holds that life may emerge from matter organized in particular ways but rejects the idea that "life is somehow hidden in matter and just waiting to manifest itself." Life is thus one possible outcome of materiality, but it is certainly not a "normal" or "expected" one—indeed, it is highly improbable, not the rule but the exception.[22] In this way, the arche-materiality of the structure of succession, of what Derrida calls "living-on," allows, as Hägglund puts it, "for a conceptual distinction between life and matter that takes into account the Darwinian explanation of how the living evolved out of the non-living, while asserting a distinguishing characteristic of life that does not make any concessions to vitalism."[23]

I'll return to the importance of this point for the question of "biologistic continuism" below, but for now I want to note a separate but related problem in Esposito's thinking about "life": the slippage in and around the term "species," which appears to be symptomatic of Esposito's desire to hold this problem of vitalism at bay without falling back into the lexicon of the "person" as the locus of the norm.

Esposito argues that the specific place where the immunitary logic operates in biopolitics is "at the juncture between the spheres of the individual and the species. When Foucault identifies the object of biopower as the population . . . he is referring to the only element that groups all individuals together into the same species: namely, the fact that they have a body. Biopolitics addresses itself to this body—an individual one because it belongs to each person, and at the same time a general one because it relates to an entire genus."[24] But if the entire point of an affirmative biopolitics for Esposito is to realize the force of "'life, singular and impersonal,'" that "cannot but resist whatever power, or knowledge, is arranged to divide it," that thus produces "new knowledge and new power as a function of its own quantitative and qualitative expansion," then it is not clear how the call of an affirmative biopolitics can be "for a new alliance between the life of the individual and the life of the *species*," since such "life" forces clearly don't stop at the water's edge of species and are instead operative at—and in fact, beneath—the level of "flesh."[25] To put it another way, "species" here cannot do any heavy lifting for Esposito, for the very same reasons that "the body" cannot be cordoned off from the "flesh"—indeed, "life," if anything, radicalizes the logic of the flesh, the being in common of embodied beings that cannot be limited to *Homo sapiens*, either philosophically or, as we have already seen, pragmatically. To put it another way, Esposito may be right that the body is the immunitary site on which biopolitics seizes control over life,[26] but the cordoning off of "the body" within the domain of "species" simply reinstates the very autoimmunitary, thanatological movement that his affirmative biopolitics wants to resist. What is needed here, then—and this will be a central intervention in the pages that follow—is a third way, one that can think life and norm together, without falling back on either the lexicon of "the person" or, at the other extreme, the radically dedifferentiating discourse of "life" which is unworkable both philosophically and pragmatically.

So the problem is not Esposito's insistence—quite correct, in my view—that "what we call the subject, or person, is nothing but the result, always provisory, of a process of individuation, or subjectification, quite irreducible to the individual and his masks," nor is it his core argument that for an affirmative biopolitics, "there can be nothing but a clear distancing from the hierarchical and exclusionary apparatus of the category of the person, in any of its declensions, theological, juridical, or philosophical."[27] It is rather that the only alternative that Esposito seems to be able to imagine to this indexing of biopolitical norms is simply its other extreme, a sort of neovitalism that ends up radically dedifferentiating the field of "the living" into a molecular wash of singularities that all equally manifest "life." And so, as Thacker notes, "the concept of life—and whether such a concept is possible—places philosophy in a hovering, wavering space between an onto-theology and an onto-biology."[28] Against this backdrop, one might well wonder about the dangers of this attraction toward "life," and not just in US political culture (with its endless warring between "pro-choice" and "pro-life" factions, for example). Indeed, were one to press the point about "onto-theology," one might well ask if it is possible, as more than one observer has noted, that a certain Christian and even Catholic thematics continues to play itself out here? Lorenzo Chiesa, for example, finds in Esposito's affirmative biopolitics a kind of secularization, if you will, of the deeply theological and Christian orientation that is quite explicit in Agamben, only here, "a life that creates and brings forth what it is not itself" is associated not with the "human" properly understood but with the "life" that is by definition not identical with its manifestations in "the living"—otherwise, after all, how could all forms of life be equal, how could "the quantitative and qualitative expansion" of life be an unmixed good?[29]

Be that as it may, Esposito's position, pragmatically speaking, fares no better. First, it replays all the quandaries around biocentrism brought to light during the 1970s and 1980s in North America during the heyday of the deep ecology movement—debates that Esposito (or for that matter his fellow Italian political philosophers) would have little reason, perhaps, to know about. As Tim Luke notes, if all forms of life are given equal value, then we face questions such as the following: "Will we allow anthrax or cholera microbes to attain self-realization in wiping out sheep herds or human kindergartens? Will we continue to deny salmonella or botulism micro-organisms their equal rights when we process the dead carcasses of animals and plants that we eat?"[30] In the face of such challenges, all that Esposito can offer is to retrofit Spinoza's concept of natural right to make "the norm the principle of unlimited equivalence for every single form of life."[31] The general idea here—and I will return to it in more detail in a moment—seems to be that this new norm will operate as a sort of homeostatic mechanism balancing the creative flourishing of various life forms. As Esposito characterizes it, "the juridical order as a whole is the product of this plurality of norms and the provisional result of their mutual equilibrium," and for this reason no "normative criterion upon which exclusionary measures" could be based is possible.[32] But such a position—and its key markers in the foregoing quotation are "plurality" and "equilibrium"—is in essence no different from deep ecology's guiding principles of biocentrism (or, in a slightly more refined version that Esposito would be forced to reject, biodiversity).

There are perhaps those who would respond to Luke's foregoing questions in the affirmative—who would argue that, yes, all forms of life should be equally allowed to take their course, even if it means a massive die-off of the species *Homo sapiens*. But biopolitically speaking, that hardly solves the problem, of course, because when we ask what the demographic distribution of such an event would likely be, we realize that the brunt would surely be absorbed by largely black and brown poor populations of the south, while those in the "rich North Atlantic democracies" (to use Richard Rorty's no-nonsense phrase) who could afford to protect themselves would surely do so.[33] And even privileging biodiversity, which would seem in tune with the "qualitative and quantitative expansion" of life that Esposito values, is equally question-begging because, as Luke notes, that means that rare species and endangered individuals are by definition more valuable than those that are more common (and this is only thinking for the moment on the level of the creature, not of the microorganism), so that, for example, given a choice between saving a California condor and a human child, one would be obliged to choose the former.[34] Thus biocentrism, as Patrick Curry observes, "is both intellectually and metaphysically implausible," and it is also "hopelessly impractical as a guide to action; you cannot ask anyone (let alone everyone) to live as if literally every life-form—a lethal virus, say—has equal value to all the others."[35]

A further problem with equating the norm with "the principle of unlimited equivalence" of life pure and simple is underscored by a prominent contemporary development that only foregrounds what was already true with regard to the "framing" of life via technology: namely, synthetic biology. As one recent article puts it, "post-genomic biology—biology 2.0, if you like—has finally killed the idea of vitalism."[36] In fact, the recent explosion of new developments in the field has depended in no small part on two factors: more and more widely accessible computing power of considerable magnitude and, more importantly, the rapidly falling costs of DNA sequencing. For example, the human genome sequenced by the Human Genome Sequencing Consortium took thirteen years and cost $3 billion; now, using the latest technology, the same work can be done in eight days at a cost of about $10,000—a figure that is sure to be even lower as you read these words. And projections are that three years from now the same work will take about fifteen minutes and cost about $1,000.[37] When, with much media fanfare, Craig Ventner and Hamilton Smith reported on May 20, 2010, in *Science* magazine that they had created a living creature with no ancestor from scratch, using off-the-shelf laboratory chemicals—a bacterium of the family *M. genitalium*—it seemed perverse to some, and analogies with Mary Shelley's *Frankenstein* were ready at hand.[38] And it perhaps seemed even more perverse when Ventner and his team added some DNA designed from scratch to "watermark" the organism with a cipher that contains the URL of a website and three quotations.[39] As many scientists point out, however, for all of its pathbreaking possibilities, synthetic biology is quite continuous with the enfolding of life and technology that reaches back hundreds, if not thousands, of years.[40]

Precisely here, it seems to me, it is worth remembering the sort of point made by Derrida in his discussion of cloning in *Rogues*. As he observes, those who oppose cloning object to it in the name of "the *nonrepetitive* unicity of the human person," the "incalculable element" of "a unique, irreplaceable, free, and thus nonprogrammable living being."[41] But what is overlooked here, he argues, is that

> so-called identificatory repetition, the duplication, that one claims to reject with horrified indignation, is already, and fortunately, present and at work everywhere it is a question of reproduction and of heritage, in culture, knowledge, language, education, and so on, whose very condi-

tions, whose production and reproduction, are assured by this duplication. . . . This is yet another way of ignoring what history, whether individual or not, owes to culture, society, education, and the symbolic, to the incalculable and the aleatory—so many dimensions that are irreducible, even for "identical" twins, to this supposedly simple, genetic naturalness. What is the consequence of all of this? That, in the end, this so-called ethical or humanist axiomatic actually shares with the axiomatic it claims to oppose a certain geneticism or biologism, indeed a deep zoologism, a fundamental but unacknowledged reductionism.[42]

Derrida's commentary here—and the example of synthetic biology in general—enables us to see how the biopolitical frame makes possible the thinking of a more nuanced and differentiated set of ethical and political relations with regard to "forms of life," but only if we do not succumb to the sort of neovitalism that, at the end of *Bios*, seems to leave us with a stark choice: either "life" and an "affirmative" biocentrism on the one hand, or, on the other, the autoimmune disorder which is bound to eventuate if the continuum of life is broken.

VI.

Claire Colebrook observes of contemporary forms of thought that seem (but only seem) to be antihumanist in their recourse to "life," "in place of man as a body with the additional capacity for reason, one distributes reason or thinking throughout life"—a fitting description, I would suggest, of Esposito's vitalistic principle that makes all forms of life equal because they equally express it. But however antihumanist such a position might appear, it is possible, Colebrook suggests, "to see such a dethroning of humanity as making way for the creation of *man*" as "one aspect of a mindful, creative, self-organising life," an expression of it "no longer detached from the world as some distinct substance or ghost in the machine—for life is now the milieu from which he emerges and through which he can read the enigmatic density of his own being."[1] Colebrook's diagnosis is certainly right as far as it goes, but what needs to be added here is Derrida's reminder that no such "reading" is available to "man." Moreover—and this is the equally radical insight we will explore in more detail in a moment—that unavailability, which is a product of the technicity or "*machinalité*" of even the most rudimentary semiotic systems constituted as they are by trace and spacing, binds the human to (at least some) nonhuman animals in their shared subjection to an "archematerialy" on the basis of which (and only on the basis of which) living beings can engage in communication and social relations at all.[2] This shared prosthetic relation to a fundamental "identificatory repetition" engenders the possibility of "reading" and "response," even as it decisively undermines and contaminates the juridical distinction between "response" and mere mechanisitic or instinctive "reaction"—a distinction that, as Derrida shows, has anchored the ontological hierarchy of human and animal in the philosophical tradition. Because of the contamination, "response" cannot accomplish the ontological work that the philosophical tradition thinks it does (and if it did, it would generate the "autoimmune" disorder that results from both anthro- and androcentrism, as Derrida argues in his later work). So the challenge we face here is to pay attention to this shared, structuring system of subjectification for both humans and (at least some) animals, while at the same time drawing out the specificity and heterogeneity of different "forms of life" as those bear on the question of norms.

One of Derrida's more well-known discussions of the respond/react opposition as it anchors the human/animal hierarchy in the Western philosophical tradition is his discussion of Lacan in *The Animal That Therefore I Am*. I have discussed this text in some detail elsewhere, but to briefly recapitulate Derrida's argument here: Lacan wants, as he notes, to reserve for the human alone the capacity to "respond" rather than simply "react" (as in, for example, a stimulus-response model).[3] Lacan concedes that some animals seem to be able not simply to react but also to respond—as in the well-known distraction displays among some species of birds. But only humans, Lacan argues, can feign feigning; only humans can lie by telling the truth. As Derrida notes, however, "it seems difficult in the first place to identify or determine a limit, that is to say an indivisible threshold between pretense and pretense of pretense."[4] "How could one distinguish," he continues,

> for example in the most elementary sexual parade or mating game, between a feint and a feint of a feint? If it is impossible to provide the criterion for such a distinction, one can conclude that every pretense of pretense remains a simple pretense (animal or imaginary, in Lacan's terms), or else, on the contrary, and just as likely, the every pretense, however simple it may be, gets repeated and reposited undecidably, in its possibility, as pretense of pretense (human or symbolic in Lacan's terms). . . . Pretense presupposes taking the other into account; it therefore supposes, simultaneously, the pretense of pretense—a simple supplementary move by the other within the strategy of the game. That supplementarity is at work from the moment of the first pretense.[5]

Moreover, as he notes—technically and decisively—"it is difficult, as Lacan does, to reserve the differentiality of signs for human language only, as opposed to animal coding. What he attributes to signs that, 'in a language' understood as belonging to the human order, 'take on their value from their relations to each other' and so on, and not just from the 'fixed correlation' between signs and reality, can and must be accorded to any code, animal or human."[6] Derrida's point here is not, of course, that humans and animals are "the same." Rather, his point is that it is

> less a matter of asking whether one has the right to refuse the animal such and such a power . . . than of asking whether what calls itself human has the right to rigorously attribute to man . . . what he refuses the animal, and whether he can ever possess the *pure, rigorous, indivisible* concept, as such, of that attribution. Thus, were we even to suppose—something I am not ready to concede—that the "animal" were incapable of covering its tracks, by what right could one concede that power to the human, to the "subject of the signifier?"[7]

Derrida develops this argument in several different registers in the seminars collected in volume 1 of *The Beast and the Sovereign*. One particularly notable example is his sometimes dizzying, often humorous exploration in seminars 5, 6, and 7 of the relations between the French words *bête* (or "beast") and *bêtise* (a word difficult to translate exactly, but idiomatic expressions in English such as "screw up" or "make an ass of oneself" would capture something of the sense). There, hard on the heels of his engagement with Lacan, he digs into Deleuze's contention in *Difference and Repetition* that "*bêtise* is not animality. The animal is guaranteed by specific forms which prevent it from being '*bête*.'"[8] For Deleuze, Derrida explains, "the animal cannot be *bête* because it is not free and has no will."[9] And this is why, Derrida writes, for Deleuze, "cruel bestiality and *bêtise* are proper to man and cannot be attributed to so-called animal beasts." And this means, in turn, that beasts "have no relation to the law" because, without free will, they cannot be held to be either cruel or responsible— that is to say, "free and sovereign," which is "the very definition of the juridical person, as a free and responsible person, able to say or imply

'I, me.'"[10] The problem with Deleuze's position, like Lacan's—and it is an odd problem indeed, given Deleuze's other philosophical commitments—is that it makes *bêtise* "a thing of the 'Me' or the 'I,'" and not "*something like a form of psychic life . . . that would not have the figure of the 'I.*'"[11]

One name for such a "form of psychic life," of course, is the "unconscious," but as Derrida is quick to note, we don't need to endorse this concept, or even Freudianism generally, to "avoid reducing the whole of psychic or phenomenological experience to its egological form," to acknowledge that "in psychic or phenomenological experience, in the self-relation of the living being, there is some non-ego." Freud or no Freud, psychoanalysis or no psychoanalysis, "it suffices," he concludes, "to admit that the living being is divisible and constituted by a multiplicity of agencies, forces, and intensities that are sometimes in tension or even in contradiction"—surely a Deleuzean point, no?[12] The point here is double: staking as Lacan and Deleuze do "everything on a sovereignty of the responsible human Me, capable of responding freely, and not only of reacting," and inscribing a *juridical* distinction "between responsible response and irresponsible reaction, and thus between sovereignty and non-sovereignty, freedom and unfreedom, as the difference between man and beast" precludes the possibility of taking seriously everything associated with the term "unconscious."[13]

Of course, as my Lacanian friends would no doubt suggest, it is worth asking whether at this moment Derrida himself is engaged in the performativity of his own *bêtise* vis-à-vis his relationship to Lacan, whether his own discourse is not betraying its own "unconscious." For as Lydia Liu among others has suggested,[14] what would seem to be a point of *contact* between Lacan and Derrida is this insistence on the radical *machinalité* of the tail that wags the dog of the Ego-subject, whether we call that tail the unconscious, the trace, or a combination of both in which it is not possible—never was possible—to unscramble the egg and separate the ego from what surrounds and indeed overdetermines it. In this light, it is perhaps symptomatic that Derrida notes of Lacan's juridical distinction between "respond" and "react"—or, more precisely, "feint" and "feigned feint"—that this "can come as a surprise in a discourse held in the name of psycho-analysis and a return to Freud."[15]

But be that as it may, we don't need the term "unconscious" or even, in the end, psychoanalysis per se, to see how the respond/react opposition cannot be maintained with the rigor that has tradition-ally secured the uncontaminated purity and singularity not of the "human" but more precisely, as Derrida puts it, of "what calls *itself* man."[16] Derrida's point here is a very simple but very powerful one:

> It suffices as a minimal requisite to take into account the divisibility, multiplicity, or difference of forces of a living being, whatever it be, in order to admit that there is no finite living being (a-human or human) which is not structured by the force-differential between which a ten-sion, if not a contradiction, is bound to localize—or localize within itself—different agencies. . . . And in these antagonisms made possible, in every finite living being, by differences of force or intensity, *bêtise* is *always necessarily on both sides, the side of the "who" and the side of the "what."*[17]

Although Derrida's discussion of the respond/react opposition does not draw in any detail on the "zoological knowledge" that he finds rather lacking in Heidegger's famous discussion of the animal as "poor in world,"[18] I believe the lines of relation between his articula-tion of the problem and contemporary research in philosophy of mind, cognitive ethology, and animal communication are quite direct, and can be framed in the materialistic and naturalistic terms we invoked earlier. Indeed, this body of research suggests that what we think of as the capacity to "respond" is the product of a complex, dynamic, mu-tually imbricated relationship between the "who" and the "what"—a fact that applies to both humans and (at least some) nonhuman ani-mals. Consider, for example, Vinciane Despret's articulation of what she calls "anthropo-zoo-genesis." In a famous experiment conducted by Robert Rosenthal to show how laboratory researchers unduly in-fluence experimental data, two groups of college students were given rats to run through various mazes, measuring their intelligence. One group was told their rats were specially bred "smart" rats; the other group, "dull" rats. And indeed, the experimental data confirmed this;

the smart rats did well in the tests, and the dull rats did poorly. In fact, however, all sixty-five rats were from the same source—no smart rat population, no dull rats either. Rosenthal's intention was to show how objective experimental data may be corrupted and compromised by how researchers interact with their experimental animals in ways they are unaware of. But as Despret points out, the really interesting questions remain: How were the results obtained? What accounts for the differences in performance between the two groups of rats?[19]

Rosenthal gave his students a questionnaire after the fact and found that the experimenters working with the smart rats regarded them as more likable and pleasant than those working with the dull rats; and Rosenthal speculated that those working with the "smart" rats probably interacted with them more gently and encouragingly. But why? Because, Despret writes, the students, given their own transversal relations and institutional situatedness, "did everything possible, everything they could, to make what Rosenthal said be true, because it mattered for them that it was."[20] All of this confirms not, as Rosenthal thought, a hard and fast difference between "reality" and "pseudo-reality," between true results and false results;[21] rather, as Despret characterizes it, what accounts for the discrepancy in the results is a complex loop of interactions between institutional, biological, affective, and other factors that literally brings forth a new reality in and through the bodies and practices in interaction—a recursive loop, in other words, between the "who" and the "what."[22]

A concept nowhere mentioned in Despret's analysis but everywhere between the lines is "play." In his seminal text on the topic, Gordon M. Burghardt, drawing in part on recent work with mirror neurons in primates, suggests that "behavioral (physical, motoric, sensory) play may be an important developmental precursor to mental play involving rehearsal, prediction, planning, imagination, problem solving and creativity" in domains such as "language and communication, cognitive (decision-making) abilities, and emotional (empathic and 'mind-reading') processes." Language, he suggests, "which we value as the most human of all our capabilities may, ironically, be derived from gesturing and signing. Such gesturing, in turn, may have emerged from the variability attendant in social play."[23] Coming at the question of "response" from the other end of the problem, philosopher of mind José Luis Bermúdez argues in *Thinking without Words* that "the contemporary behavioral sciences have almost completely abandoned a longstanding tenet in the study of cognition, namely, that language and thought go hand in hand, and hence that the study of thought can only proceed via the study of language."[24] Moreover, he notes—and this is directly relevant to the hard association of "reacting" with animals,

> Cognitive ethologists, unlike the older generation of comparative psychologists, have little time for the project of trying to explain how an animal behaves in terms of nonrepresentational stimulus-response mechanisms or the fixed behavior patterns known as innate releasing mechanisms. They start from the assumption that animals have certain desires and certain beliefs about how the world is organized and act on the basis of those beliefs to try to ensure the satisfaction of their desires.[25]

As primatologist Barbara King has noted, those "desires" are neither purely innate nor purely individual, but depend instead on a "dynamic dance" between organism and environment, physiological wetware and semiotic machinery, the individual and the ongoing storehouse of social knowledge held by a particular group of animals. In other words, it is anything *but* a neat division between responding and reacting, between the "who" and the "what."[26] In fact, her own developmental systems theory approach reaches back to the work of Gregory Bateson and his crucial reframing of the cognizing being (human or animal) as a "*system* whose boundaries do not at all coincide with the boundaries of either the body or of what is popularly called 'the self' or 'consciousness.'"[27]

Such a view enables us to gain some critical distance on another dogma of contemporary science—not the dogma of associating cognition and mentation with language in the narrow sense alone, but the dogma of reducing the problem of consciousness to discrete neurophysiological states. As philosopher of mind Alva Noë argues in *Out of Our Heads: Why You Are Not Your Brain, and Other Lessons from the Biology of Consciousness*, much orthodoxy in recent neuroscience of consciousness is utterly continuous with the Cartesianism that its "materialism" appears to reject, when in fact "the locus of consciousness is the dynamic life of the whole, environmentally plugged-in person or animal."[28] As Noë points out, the main lesson of the biology of consciousness is not that the important questions are reducible to a biological or neurological substrate but rather that, to comprehend the phenomenon, we have to adopt a mode of thinking that does not cleave along the lines of human vs. animal, who vs. what, inside brain vs. outside world, or, for that matter, organic vs. inorganic. Only by doing so can we understand in a more robust way how humans and animals respond to their worlds—beginning, as Noë notes (with a nod toward the seminal work of Jakob von Uexküll) with the recognition that "it is not the case that all animals have a common external environment," because "to each different form of animal life there is a distinct, corresponding, ecological domain or habitat." In short, "all animals live in structured worlds."[29]

The wide-ranging implications of that apparently quite straightforward principle have been explored in some detail over the past twenty-five years by Humberto Maturana and Francisco Varela, who show that in creatures who have sufficient neurophysiological plasticity to engage in what is sometimes called "proportionate learning," this dynamic interfolding of inside and outside, organism and environment, body and semiotic machinery, gives rise to what they call *"new phenomenological domains"*;[30] "whenever they arise—if only to last for a short time—they generate a particular internal phenomenology, namely, one in which the *individual ontogenies of all the participating organisms occur fundamentally as part of the network of co-ontogenies that they bring about.*"[31] This is true even of social insects, but because of the limits placed on the concentration of neurocephalic tissue (and thus their plasticity) by their exoskeletons, their individual ontogenies are quite rigid and subject to a very limited set of variations.[32] Thus, their individual ontogenies are of little importance in explaining their behavior. For creatures of sufficient neurophysiological plasticity, however, it is a different story, one in which the correspondingly high degree of individual variation in individual ontogenies gives rise to the more complex social and communicational behaviors necessary to coordinate them.[33] We find here, as Barbara King characterizes it, the possibility of *emergent* forms of meaning that are dynamically coconstructed in social interaction.[34]

In his now-classic essays on play and communication in mammals, Gregory Bateson notes that such phenomena "could only occur if the participant organisms were capable of some degree of meta-communication, *i.e.,* of exchanging signals which would carry the message 'this is play.' The playful nip denotes the bite, but it does not denote what would be denoted by the bite" —namely real aggression.[35] Thus, Bateson concludes, "paradox is doubly present in the signals which are exchanged. . . . Not only do the playing animals not quite mean what they are saying but, also, they are usually communicating about something which does not exist."[36] What we discover here, as Bateson observes, is therefore not just the ability to signal "this is play," and to exchange signs based on a shared meta-communicative frame, but also the ability to question, to ask, "*Is* this play?" —a point whose Derridean resonance will become even clearer in a moment.[37] As philosopher of cognition and consciousness Daniel Dennett puts it, "you have to have a cognitive economy with a budget for exploration and self-stimulation to provide the space for the recursive stacks of derived desires that make fun possible. You have taken a first step when your architecture permits you to appreciate the meaning of 'Stop it, I love it!'" —a phenomenon widely observed, of course (as is Bateson's "*Is* this play?"), in both human and non-human animals.[38]

Given my criticism of Esposito's use of the concept of "species" earlier, a predictable rejoinder at this juncture would be to say that I am simply replacing anthropocentrism with "mammalism," or, beyond that, "vertebratism": simply drawing the immunological line at a slightly more extended boundary, but one still organized around classes of creatures who look a lot like "us." For the more naturalistically minded—to take that objection at its word, for the moment—I would point to what we might call the "scandal" of the cephalopods. In fact, as recent research makes clear, the kinds of questions we are exploring here around "response" can in no way be limited to the domain of the vertebrates or even, for that matter, the chordates. Gordon Burghardt draws our attention to evidence of play in the octopus, but that is just the tip of the iceberg, as it turns out.[39] Cephalopods display many of the traits—cognitive, affective, and behavioral—that we consider the exclusive domain of the "higher" vertebrates; they are known for their curiosity, even mischievousness, and appear to engage in foresight, planning, deception, and even rudimentary tool use.[40] In captivity, they readily solve problems they would never encounter in the wild (such as removing the lid from a jar to obtain the food inside), they appear to have distinctive personalities, and it has even been suggested that they may experience REM sleep and something akin to dreaming. But the scandal of the cephalopods extends even further. Not only do they challenge the deep-seated idea that intelligence advanced in a simple linear fashion from fish to amphibians and reptiles, and then to birds, mammals, through early primates and finally to humans, they also force us to rethink the assumption that such capacities can only evolve in creatures with a relatively long life-span and who live in complex social groups. After all, most cephalopods live only for about a year, and the longest-lived, the giant Pacific octopus, lives only four years; moreover, the social lives of squid and cuttlefish are rudimentary to nonexistent, and the octopus itself is solitary.[41] The scandal of the cephalopods—a scandal, that is, only if you are a "mammalist" or "vertebratist"—leaves us with an important lesson: that the capacity to respond should not be linked to generic biological markers, such as membership in a particular species or phylum. Indeed, that would be simply another version of the work that "race" has done in the biopolitical paradigm.

biologistic continuism

VII.

What begins to dawn on us at this point, then, is the full complexity
of the confrontation with "biologistic continuism" as articulated by
Derrida, which assumes its most challenging and illuminating form in
his reading of Heidegger.[1] Heidegger was right, Derrida argues, to reject the idea of "some homogeneous continuity between what calls *itself* man and what *he* calls the animal," and he was also right to insist
that the fundamental questions here are not biological but, if you like,
phenomenological if not indeed ontological (though Derrida's caveat
of "what calls *itself* man" would eventually challenge that last characterization).[2] And Heidegger was also right, as Dominick LaCapra
observes, in his "departure from Husserl's attempt to center philosophy on the intentional consciousness of the meaning-generating, radically constructivist ego or subject," and his increasing emphasis on
understanding "human being in relation to Being and not vice versa,"
a project in which "the dignity of the human being is enhanced if it is
seen within a larger relational network that is not unproblematically
centered on human freedom or human interests."[3] What Heidegger
was *wrong* about, Derrida argues, was his insistence that whatever is
at stake here—phenomenologically, ontologically, ethically—corre-
sponds to a difference *in kind*, an absolute limit, between "*the* human"
and "*the* animal" (which is why Derrida calls it, precisely, a dogma).[4]
Derrida's position, on the other hand, will consist "not in effacing the
limit" between different forms of life "but in multiplying its figures, in
complicating, thickening, delinearizing, folding, and dividing the line
precisely by making it increase and multiply."[5] And here the problems
with the headlong rush toward "life" that we find late in Esposito's
Bios come fully into view; the problem is that vast differences between

the orangutan, the wasp, and the kudzu plant—Derrida even calls them "abysses," but they are abysses that, unlike Heidegger, apply *within* the "animal" kingdom[6]—fall out because those differences are all reduced to the same *kind* of difference.

Not one line, then, but many. But not "no line" either, and a further way of "delinearizing" it is to realize that the material processes—some organic, some not—that give rise to different ways of responding to the world for different living beings are radically asynchronous, moving at different speeds, from the glacial pace of evolutionary adaptations and mutations to the fast dynamics of learning and communication that, through neurophysiological plasticity, literally rewire biological wetware. In this light, it is clear, as Matthew Calarco puts it, that "the presubjective conditions that give rise to human subjectivity" cannot be restricted to humans alone. Instead, the more fundamental issue is the "complex networks of relations, affects, and becomings into which both human beings and animals are thrown. As such, posthumanism is confronted with the necessity of returning to first philosophy with the task of creating a nonanthropocentric ontology of life-death." This does not mean that whoever is the addressee here—human or nonhuman—is defined by the "transcendence" of the biological; the point is rather that everything that *is* relevant here applies in ways that have nothing to do with species designation and, moreover, operates in a way that is not wholly reducible to the facticity of biological existence, either "human" or "animal." Paradoxically, then, the rejection of "biologistic continuism" in fact makes possible a more robust naturalistic account of the processes that give rise to that which cannot be reduced to the biological alone—or even, more radically still, to the organic per se. For as Derrida notes in a late interview, "beginning with *Of Grammatology*, the elaboration of a new concept of the trace had to be extended to the entire field of the living, or rather to the life/death relation," and it is by virtue of the trace and its technicity that both humans and (at least some) animals are "thrown."[8]

The importance of this point cannot be overstressed, for it is here that the radically ahuman character of what Heidegger called Dasein in relation to technicity and temporality reenters the picture, and in a manner that in no way can be rigorously reserved for the "human" versus the "animal." There are both logically and ontologically inflected versions of this claim. Martin Hägglund frames the former by arguing that Derrida's articulation of the trace is not "an assertion about the nature of being as such" but rather a "*logical structure* that makes explicit what is implicit in the concept of succession." This is not "to oppose it to ontology, epistemology or phenomenology, but to insist that the trace is a metatheoretical notion that elucidates what is entailed by a commitment to succession in either of these registers."[9] As for the more ontological version, Richard Beardsworth notes that when Heidegger thinks Dasein in terms of time, he avoids confronting this constitutive aporia "by thinking time in oppositional terms, those of 'vulgar' and the 'primordial' temporalization." Such a move "betrays a repetition of metaphysical logic at the very moment that Heidegger wishes to destroy logic," however, and it prevents Heidegger, "paradoxically, from thinking the 'there' (*da*) of 'Dasein.'"[10] But as for the "there" of Dasein, there is, to paraphrase Gertrude Stein, no "there" there, for as Hägglund puts it, "*time is nothing in itself*;" nothing but "the negativity that is intrinsic to succession." Thus, "time cannot be anything or do anything without a spatialization that constrains the power of the virtual in making it dependent on material conditions."[11] Those "material conditions," of course, are constituted by the "*machinalité*" or technicity of the trace in the most general sense—a sense that is not limited, of course, either to technology in a strict sense or to human beings alone. As Beardsworth puts it, following Bernard Stiegler (and beyond that, André Leroi-Gourhan), "technical objects constitute the very process of Dasein's experiencing of time, that is, of remembering and anticipating"—a more specific manifestation of what Hägglund calls "succession." "Without memory support systems," Beardsworth continues, "there would be no experience of the past and nothing from which to 'select' in order to invent the future." And so, he concludes, "Heidegger's phantasmatic opposition in *Being and Time* between primordial temporality and vulgar time is a metaphysical disavowal of the *originary technicity* of the 'there' of time."[12]

To emphasize Stiegler's relationship to anthropologist Leroi-Gourhan rather than to Derrida is to foreground the ontological rather than logical version of the argument. As David Wills elegantly sums up the trajectory of Leroi-Gourhan's work, the hominid mutation to the upright stance that frees the hand and makes the face available for language "inscribes a definition of the human that is utterly determined by the idea of exteriorization, the hand reaching outside the body to enter into a prosthetic relation with the tool, the mouth producing or adopting the prosthetic device that is language. As a result, the archive is born, the human species begins to develop a memory bank, and its relation to time begins to be catalogued by means of the traces of an artificial memory."[13] As Stiegler argues, we can now imagine "an analytic of the temporal being that is Dasein, of the *who* that would be an analytic of the *prostheticity* whereby he exists and becomes embodied—of prostheticity *qua* being his already-there, or of his *already-there* qua being *essentially* prosthetic (accidental), never manifesting itself other than as a *what*."[14]

It is well beyond my scope here to parse the complex way in which this dynamic relates to the question of species in Stiegler (and, beyond that, in Leroi-Gourhan).[15] But there can be little doubt that the essential relation of the "who" and the "what" as described by Stiegler is true of populations of at least some kinds of nonhuman animals who engage in complex forms of social communication and who live in groups where there are well-recorded differences in culturally specific behaviors.[16] Though there is no doubt a vast qualitative difference between the developing modes of human exteriorization and "grammatization" and those of other species—a point on which both Derrida and Stiegler would agree—the animal behaviors and forms of communication we have been discussing are "already-there," forming an exteriority, an "elsewhere," that enables some animals more than others to "differentiate" and "individuate" their existence—and thus to be "thrown"—in a manner *only possible* on the basis of a complex interplay of the "who" and the "what," the individual's "embodied enaction" (to use Maturana and Varela's phrase) and exteriority of the material and semiotic technicities that interact with and rewire it, leading to highly variable ontogenies, complex forms of social interaction, individual personalities, and so on.[17] Regarding the differences between the tool and "phonetic or graphic symbols" as forms of exteriority and technicity, Stiegler himself makes the point well that "Derrida will draw the grammatological consequences," with the idea of the "arche-trace . . . allowing the ensemble of the movement of exteriorization to be interpreted as différance."[18] As Derrida asserts in the passage referenced by Stiegler,

> If the expression ventured by Leroi-Gourhan is accepted, one could speak of a "liberation of memory," of an exteriorization always already begun but always larger than the trace which, beginning from the elementary programs of so-called "instinctive" behavior up to the constitution of electronic card-indexes and reading machines, enlarges differance [sic] and the possibility of putting in reserve: it at once and in the same movement constitutes and effaces so-called conscious subjectivity.[19]

What this means, then, is that the exteriority and technicity on the basis of which "intentionality" and the "subject" arise as an effect of "putting in reserve" are *double*—not just of the prostheticity of tool and semiotic code through which communication and culture take place, but also of "the notion of *program*" and the "instinctive" behaviors of "reacting" whose "movement goes far beyond the possibilities of the 'intentional consciousness'"—a dynamic that obtains, of course, for both human and nonhuman animals.[20]

Indeed, as scholars such as Burghardt and Mike Hansell remind us, the dynamics at work here involve an extremely complex interplay of genetic, physiological, adaptive, environmental, and social factors that determine how animals respond to their environments and to each other.[21] As Barbara King describes this process in her work with great apes,

> Apes' distinct selves emerge developmentally, as do children's, through a fluid dynamic among processes rooted in biology and others in culture. Genes matter, brains matter, bodies matter, and social processes of engagement matter, and indeed genes and brains and bodies and social processes co-construct each other. . . .
>
> This three-way intersection, and the developmental dynamics that I highlight as part of it, occurs robustly across the various species of great apes, even as it varies in terms of quality when expressed in individual lives. Flexible meaning-making spans the various environments, wild and captivity, in which modern-day apes live. This very robustness makes it likely that flexible meaning-making has been phylogenetically conserved, i.e., that it was present in the common ancestor of great apes and hominids. . . .

That behavioral plasticity, at both the population and individual level, is part of our evolutionary history is serious news. What does it mean? It means that apes focus our gaze on plasticity and contingency rather than on innatism or essentialized adaptation to a supposed "ancestral environment." This recognition not only de-centers the human, it also de-centers the idea that human behaviors (and human thought patterns) are highly constrained by our past.[22]

The rearticulation of the "facticity" and "nullity" of Dasein in terms of "originary prostheticity"[23] makes it clear why one of the more ingenious humanist responses to the "delinearizing" of the line between forms of life that I have been mapping is finally unsatisfactory: namely, the response that the distinctly human is constituted precisely by a radical *not* being-able that is barred to other creatures: in Heidegger, the "letting be of Being" (but also, in a different register, the existential of Being-toward-death);[24] in Agamben, Dasein as that being who has "awakened *from* its own captivation *to* its own captivation. The awakening of the living being to its own being-captivated, the anxious and resolute opening to a not-open";[25] in Žižek, the "self-hindering" subject constituted by a internally blocked relation to the Real qua body which it then projects outward in a variety of symptomatic reactions to its own impossibility, its own "wound."[26] As Derrida points out, however, this essential "(not) being-able" is not the prerogative or even the place, you might say, of either the subject or indeed of "the human," since it is to be located elsewhere, in an alterity that is not just radically extrasubjective, and not just radically ahuman, but also, in fact, radically *inorganic*: namely, in the prosthetic relation to the externality and technicity of trace, archive, symbolic system or semiotic code, however rudimentary. The subject, in other words, comes into being only by virtue of what it is not—what it is *radically* and *absolutely* not—rather than by virtue of something it *chooses* not to be (even in the mode of misrecognition, as Lacan et al. would have it), something over which—either through intentionality or unconscious disavowal—it has appropriative power.[27] The "not-human" of Dasein may thus be understood anew, and, in this light, LaCapra's suggestion that "it is at least conceivable that nonhumans are *Dasein*" is less improbable than it might at first appear.[28] For as he observes, Dasein is "a being marked by language . . . and an internally self-contestatory relation to world-disclosure (or the open)"; it is "a site for an inquiry into Being as an open relational network (later evoked in Derrida's often misunderstood notion of a general text or trace-structure) in which the being in question is always already implicated."[29]

Indeed, in light of this reconceptualization of the nonplace or not-"there" of Dasein, we might even say that Heidegger's designation of animals as "having a world in the mode of not-having" is in fact the most adequate description of Dasein that we are likely to come up with.[30] This is not to say, of course, that humans and nonhuman animals are "the same," nor is it to say that animals are more "in" Dasein than human beings. It is simply to say that no rigorous line can be drawn between humans and animals in relation to the question of Dasein. As David Farrell Krell notes in his seminal study *Daimon Life: Heidegger and Life Philosophy*, Heidegger "tries to reduce the *Offensein* [openness] of animality to its enclosure with a ring of disinhibitions, of passive subjections and preprogrammed responses . . . a closed circle of benumbed behavior (*Benommensein*)," yet that circle is "continually undone" by "something like *time*, and something very much like *death*."[31] In fact, Krell argues,

> I would stress far more than he [Derrida] does the fact that Heidegger uses the very same word to describe the world-relation of animals and the appropriate comportment toward being that characterizes Dasein: if the lizard sunning itself on a rock is benumbed (*benommen*), so is Dasein, not only when it succumbs to the world's distractions and goes sunbathing but also precisely when it confronts the uncanniness of its existence in anxiety. Appropriate Dasein, rapt to the ownmost possibility of its existence, is an animal."[32]

So it is that death "shatters" the ring of disinhibitions "and signals the way in which time—the marking of time—always bears a fundamental relation to the animal's life. The animal is thrown. . . , cast into its life and projected toward death as no stone is ever thrown."[33] But this first form of finitude is redoubled by a second; if having a world "as such and in its being" is impossible, it is precisely because the fundamental structure and systematicity of trace and spacing is the "not-having," the second form of finitude, that makes such "having" possible in the first place. As Derrida suggests in his discussion of Heidegger in *The Animal That Therefore I Am*, the "question of finitude will traverse the entire seminar,"[34] but the virtue of focusing on Heidegger's break with biologistic continuism here, his insistence that "the determination regarding life . . . is not essential in order to determine the *Dasein*,"[35] is to draw our attention to what I have elsewhere called the importance of this "double finitude": not just the finitude of being an embodied, mortal being, of "being toward death," but also a second kind of finitude—the radical exteriority and technicity of any semiotic system—that makes that first form of finitude *inappropriable* and unavailable to us (since, strictly speaking, "it"'s concept cannot be said to be "ours" alone).[36]

To unpack this claim that "having a world in the mode of not-having" that is associated by Heidegger with animals *is* the most fitting description of Dasein we are likely to come up with, we will have to connect the dots in an extraordinarily suggestive but also extraordinarily elliptical passageway in Derrida's engagement with Heidegger, one that involves a sort of reconjugation by Derrida himself of the relationship between two of his own texts separated by nearly twenty years: *Of Spirit: Heidegger and the Question* (1987, translated 1989), and *The Animal That Therefore I Am* (2006, translated 2008). And it is a reconjugation, moreover, that takes place largely on the basis of endnotes put in conversation with each other. In the opening essay of *The Animal That Therefore I Am*, Derrida quotes a footnote in *Of Spirit* regarding "the gnawing, ruminant, and silent voracity" of what he calls "an animal-machine," "an animal-machine of reading and rewriting," one that would cross out and put under erasure terms in Heidegger's corpus such as "Being," "spirit," and so on. Why "animal?" Because it is associated in Heidegger's discourse and in Western philosophy generally not with responding but with reacting, with automaticity. "This animal-machine," he continues, "has a family resemblance to the virus," "neither animal nor nonanimal, neither organic nor inorganic, neither living nor dead." He continues: "This quasi-animal would no longer have to relate itself to being *as such* (something Heidegger thinks the animal is incapable of), since it would take into account the need to strike out 'being.' But as a result, in striking out 'being' and taking itself beyond or on this side of the question (and hence of the response) is it something completely other than a species of animal?"[37] Clearly, the answer is "yes," because this "animal-machine" refers to nothing other than the "double finitude" and its trace-structure that we have been discussing, that which traverses "the life/death relation"; that is why it takes account of "the need to strike out 'being.'"[38]

Here, as Derrida shows in the extraordinary seven-and-a-half-page footnote in *Of Spirit*'s last pages, he is tracing or "tracking," as he would say in the more recent text, the implicit logic of the late Heidegger's concept of *Zusage* (translated variously as "promise, agreement or consent, originary abandonment to what is given in the promise itself"), which is an "acquiescence" or a "*yes*" that precedes all language.[39] "It is in the name of this *Zusage*," Derrida writes, "that he [Heidegger] again puts in question, if one can still call it this, the ultimate authority, the supposed last instance of the questioning attitude" (and here we should be reminded of the entire discourse in Heidegger, developed by Derrida, Cavell, and others, of the "gift," of thought as reception and of the common root of "thinking" and "thanking").[40] In this situation, "thought is a 'listening,'" Derrida continues, and thus we must "cross through the question marks," as Heidegger puts it.[41] Now we can fast-forward to *The Animal That Therefore I Am* and its own endnote on *this* note from *Of Spirit* which we have been discussing. Here, Derrida asks us "to dream of what the Heideggerian corpus would look like on the day when, with all the application and consistency required, the operations prescribed by him" would be carried out—all those operations of crossing out, marking through, erasing, or putting in or out of quotation marks such terms as "spirit."[42] Would such a language, without the question,

> this language "before" the question, this language of the *Zusage* (acquiescence, affirmation, agreement, etc.), therefore be a language without a response? A "moment" of language that is in its essence released from all relation to an expected response? But if one links the concept of the animal . . . to the double im-possibility, the double incapacity of question and response, is it because the "moment," the instance and possibility of the *Zusage* belong to an "experience" of language about which

one could say, even if it is not in itself "animal," that it is not something that the "animal" could be deprived of? That would be enough to de-stabilize a whole tradition, to deprive it of its fundamental argument.[43]

We are now in a better position to fully grasp the biopolitical point of Derrida's observation in the "Eating Well" interview that "the power to ask questions," which "in the end, is how Heidegger defines the *Dasein*," may be seen as anterior— "before"—the question of the subject, of the "who" for whom and to whom we are responsible, but only to give way to "another possibility," a more fundamental one that "overwhelms the question itself, re-inscribes it in the experience of an 'affirmation,' of a 'yes' or of an 'en-gage' . . . that 'yes, yes' that answers before even being able to formulate a question, that is respon-sible without autonomy, before and in view of all possible autonomy of the who-subject."[44] "Not only is the obligation not lessened in this situation," Derrida continues, "but, on the contrary, it finds in it its only possibility, which is neither subjective nor human. Which doesn't mean that it is inhuman or without subject, but that it is out of this dislocated *affirmation* . . . that something like the subject, man, or whoever it might be can take shape." "*Whoever it might be.*"[45]

Why "without autonomy"? Because this originary "yes," as Mar-tin Hägglund puts it, "answers to the trace structure of time that is the condition for life in general."[46] That is to say, it answers to the fact that the other is just as constitutively other to itself as I am to myself, just as constitutively prosthetic, brought into being by a technicity and spacing that is radically neither self nor other, radically nonliving. This means, in turn, that "every finite other is absolutely other, not because it is absolutely in itself," as Hägglund writes, "but on the con-trary because it can never be in itself."[47] The originary "yes" is there-fore "nothing in itself," but rather "marks the opening of an unpre-dictable future that one will have to negotiate, without any affirmative or negative response being given in advance."[48] But "life in general" is already, as I have suggested, *too* general to be of use in a biopolitical frame. Of course, there are many, many forms of life—plant life, bac-terial life, and much else—that fall outside the parameters I have been describing, at least as far as we know at the moment: indeed, the over-whelming majority of life forms on earth. But my foregrounding of the "who" here is meant to remind us that while it is no doubt worthwhile to continually rethink the relations between different forms of life, whatever they may be, and, beyond that, to understand as fully as possible the complex ways in which they are enmeshed and networked with the inorganic world (as Jane Bennett, Bruno Latour, and others have explored), the questions of ethics, law, justice, and "hospitality" pose a specific kind of challenge: namely, that in a "parliament of things" (Latour) or a "political ecology of things" (Bennett) some of those "things" are also "whos" and not just "whats"—even as *any* "who" becomes one only by virtue of also being, prosthetically, a "what."[49] Is there not a qualitative difference between the chimpanzee used in biomedical research, the flea on her skin, and the cage she lives in—and a difference that matters more (one might even say, in Derridean tones, "infinitely" more)[50] to the chimpanzee than to the flea or the cage? I think there is.

This is not to reinstate what is obviously an untenable opposition between persons and things; indeed, the prosthetic logic of the "who" and the "what" that I have been pursuing argues precisely the opposite. But it is to put our finger on a specific challenge entailed by thickening and deepening, rather than flattening, our description of the worlds and networks we share, and their qualitative dimensions—a challenge that returns us, but at a different angle of approach, to the question of biocentrism that we discussed earlier. Dale Jamieson captures something of this challenge in a now-classic essay tracing the development of environmental ethics in the 1980s. To be a card-carrying member of the environmental ethics camp, he writes, one had to hold that nonsentient entities such as ecosystems, the land, and so on had inherent value; one had to believe, more precisely, that "value is mind-independent in the following respect: even if there were no conscious beings, aspects of nature would still be inherently valuable."[51] Of course, as some of the consequences of this view became clear—for example, that individual entities, including human beings, who compromised such independent values could be readily sacrificed for the greater biotic good—even well-known supporters such as J. Baird Callicott began to abandon it.[52] The nub of the problem, as Jamieson points out, is that "the existence of valuers is a necessary condition" for those nonsentient entities to have value, which

re-evaluation of "thing-ness"

is not the same as saying that only valuers have value. "We can be sentientist with respect to the source of values," Jamieson points out, "yet non-sentientist with respect to their content. Were there no sentient beings there would be no values but it doesn't follow from this that only sentient beings are valuable."[53] The problem is summed up well by philosopher Levi Bryant, who writes that the issue is

> asking how the domain of value might be extended *beyond* the human, without humans being at the center, or all questions of value pertaining to nonhumans being questions about the *relationship* of humans to nonhumans. In other words, the litmus test . . . revolves around whether that domain of value would continue to be a domain of value *even if* humans cease to exist. That seems to be a pretty tall order or very difficult to think.

"No case could here be made," he continues, "that there's something of *intrinsic* value in nonhumans such as animals or the planets. Rather, we would be committed to the thesis that there are only *relative* values of some sort or another. . . . The planet, for example, would only take on value-predicates in relation to humans. Were humans to not exist, the planet would neither be valueless or valuable. It would just *be*."[54]

But as I have been arguing, a *third* possibility exists, which is that questions of value indeed necessarily depend on a "to whom it matters," but that "to whom" need not be—indeed, as we have already seen, *cannot* only be—human, either in the sense of excluding by definition nonhuman animals, *or* in the sense of a "human" who is not always already radically other to itself, prosthetically constituted by the ahuman and indeed inorganic. If the capacity to "respond," to be a "to whom," is not given but rather emerges, is brought forth, out of a complex and enfolded relation to the "what," to its outside (whether in the form of the environment, the other, the archive, the tool, or the "instinctive" program of behavior), then the addressee of value—and indeed of immunitary protection—is permanently open to the possibility of "whoever it might be." Here, it is worth remembering that the capacity to "respond" is quite obviously highly contextual. It's no surprise that we humans tend to be "best" at it within the parameters of the particular world that we've built for ourselves, with an eye very much *to* ourselves. But in other contexts—when we depend on the extraordinary abilities of service animals, for example, or when we find ourselves in all our long-limbed awkwardness in the ocean with dolphins or sea lions—the articulation of the "who" with the "what" is an altogether different matter.[55] Indeed, it seems entirely plausible, even likely, that the opening to the question of the "who" that has occurred over the past few decades with regard to some nonhuman animals might well extend in the future into forms of life that we as yet scarcely understand—or, to put an even finer point on it vis-à-vis the question of synthetic biology, that have yet to be invented.[56] Bryant is right, in other words, that were there no "to whom," "the planet would neither be valueless or valuable. It would just *be*." But he is wrong to assume that this hinges on whether *humans* alone exist.

From this vantage—to put it slightly otherwise—the problem with the recourse to "life" as the ethical sine qua non is that it bespeaks the desire for a nonperspectival ethics, ethics imagined fundamentally as a noncontingent view from nowhere, a view which—for that very reason—can declare all forms of life of equal value. And here, we can bring to light what is particularly problematic about Esposito's recourse to Spinozan "natural right" as the background against which he seeks to ground norms in a naturalistic basis.[57] As Esposito puts it, we find in the norm "the principle of unlimited equivalence for every single form of life"; and (following Spinoza), "the juridical order as a whole is the product of this plurality of norms and provisional result of their mutual equilibrium."[58] But the question, of course, is this: From what vantage would it be judged that the equilibrium invoked by Esposito is achieved? Spinoza's answer, as we know, was "God": each particular thing "is determined by another particular thing to exist in a certain way, yet the force by which each one perseveres in existing follows from the eternal necessity of the nature of God."[59] But, of course, as Niklas Luhmann would be the first to remind us, what "God" names here is the desire for the impossible or, at the very least (to put it a little more charitably), the premodern: an observer who can be both self-referential, contingent, socially constructed and historically specific, *and* universal and transhistorical at the same time. In other words, what is wanted here is an escape from responsibility for the inescapable fact that *all* norms are "exclusionary" simply because they are contingent (as Richard Rorty would put it), selective and self-referential (Luhmann), or, as Derrida will put it, "performative" and "conditional."

That is to say, there is no "god's eye view"; there are *only* "limited points of view." But the fact that any norm *is* unavoidably perspectival doesn't dictate relativism, solipsism, or autoimmunitary closure. Quite the contrary—and this is a point I will develop in the next section—because of its constitutive self-referential blindness (Luhmann), its constitutively "performative" and "conditional" character (Derrida), it constitutes the opening to the other and to the outside, to the necessity of other observations (Luhmann) and even to futurity or the "to come" of justice itself (Derrida). Indeed, for these very reasons, such an equilibrium is to be not desired but avoided. If there are, as Hägglund writes, "potentially an endless number of others to consider, and one cannot take any responsibility without excluding some others in favor of certain others," then "what makes it *possible* to be responsible is thus what at the same time makes it *impossible* for any responsibility to be fully responsible."[60] And for the very same reasons, an ethics of pure equilibrium without decision, without discrimination—without, in short, selection and a perspective—would be, paradoxically, unethical. It's not that we shouldn't strive for unconditional hospitality and endeavor to be fully responsible; it's simply that to do so, it is necessary to do so selectively and partially, thus conditionally, which in turn calls forth the need to be more fully responsible than we have already been.

VIII.

We are now in a better position to articulate the relationship between the "before" of the law and its addressee, "whoever it might be," antecedent to the law's historical contingency and social conventions, and the law's "after," its "conditional" and "performative" character, or what Niklas Luhmann will theorize, more restrictively still, as the law's "autopoiesis." Luhmann's work, because of its larger set of theoretical commitments—for example, his contention that the basic elements of social systems are not people but communicational events— provides a particularly stringent example of how the law is necessarily denaturalized and differentiated from any moral or naturalistic ground in the sense of a Kantian regulative Idea. Like Derrida, he would insist (but even more strongly) on the *difference* between law and justice (or what Luhmann tends to frame as questions of law versus morality). But—and this is typical, as I've argued elsewhere, of the relationship between Luhmann's work and Derrida's[1]—where Derrida would see the difference between the pragmatic immanence of legal doctrine and the question of justice as a resource or reservoir for keeping the law honest, as it were, confronting it with its own "impossibility," Luhmann's *functional* account would see that difference simply as a *problem* that the legal system must find ways to handle in terms of its own autopoiesis.

For Derrida, justice can't *simply* be the routine carrying out of the legal system's norms. As he puts it in *Rogues* (reprising one of the central points of "Force of Law"),

> Where I have at my disposal a determinable rule, I know what must be done, and as soon as such knowledge dictates the law, action follows

knowledge as a calculable consequence: one *knows* what path to take, one no longer hesitates. The decision then no longer decides anything but is made in advance and is thus in advance annulled. It is simply deployed, without delay, presently, with the automatism attributed to machines[2]

—and, ironically enough, to animals as those who can only "react" by means of an instinctive program but cannot "respond," and thus cannot act with responsibility. For Luhmann, on the other hand, the immanence and self-reference of the legal system is precisely what it *enables* it to address the problem of justice (or "morality") by changing the question, as it were, into something that can actually be answered, functionally speaking, by the law. The function of law, Luhmann argues, "does not lie in the alternative of recognizing a naturally binding minimal order or an unrestrained arbitrariness," but rather in using the schematism legal/illegal to secure the broader "autopoiesis of society's communication system as much as possible against as many disturbances produced by this system as possible."[3]

This radical "denaturalization" of the law via its own autopoietic closure decisively separates Luhmann's view from Roberto Esposito's, and it also reveals a difficulty with Bruno Latour's "political ecology"—it further denaturalizes Latour's denaturalization, you might say. Latour's political ecology makes it clear that the distinction between "life" or "nature" and their others—all their others—cannot be rigorously maintained. Instead, political ecology "dissolves boundaries and redistributes agents" across what used to be opposed ontological domains.[4] Very much along the lines of our earlier discussion of "biosocial collectivities," it multiplies "hybrid" political entities out of "actants" (both human and nonhuman), and in so doing it enables nonhuman entities to participate in the larger political process by means of their resistance and "recalcitrance." Political ecology thus becomes a process, as Latour winningly puts it, of "*collective experimentation* on the possible associations between things and people."[5]

The problem with Latour's position from the vantage systems theory, however, is that it ignores the autopoiesis of the law—and, more broadly, the phenomenon of functional differentiation, the hallmark of modernity if we believe Luhmann, of which it is a part. It ignores, in other words, how what is "before" the law and outside it in the form of "perturbations" and "resistances" is always addressed in terms of the law's "after," its own self-reference. As legal theorist Gunther Teubner puts it, Latour imagines a "great unified collective" where professions make their contributions to the decision-making process in a single conversation, but in fact there is little evidence to suggest that "an overarching societal discourse" called "political ecology" will emerge. Indeed, the phenomenon of functional differentiation suggests quite otherwise, and thus the sites on which Latour's political ecology plays out are fragmented, "dispersed over different social institutions."[6] Each social subsystem operates "under sharply defined conditions" for attributing actions, responsibilities, rights, duties, and so on.[7] "Using their specific models of rationality," Teubner writes, "each institution produces a different actor, even where concretely it is the same, human or non-human, that is involved."[8] This doesn't mean that the question of nonhuman actants—specifically, animals and electronic agents in Teubner's analysis—doesn't affect the operations of the law or of other social subsystems; it means, rather, that they affect them in a quite specific way. And it also means that these new social actors thus "lead a highly fragmented existence in society," appearing "in very different guises in politics, in the economy, in the law, and in other social contexts." Indeed, this is precisely what we have already seen in the case of companion versus food animals.[9] And thus, as Teubner puts it, the result is "not a compromise on the conditions of agency" between the various social subsystems to form a single political ecology, "but, rather, a multitude of new differences—now *within* each institution."[10] "Social systems do listen to the needs of other social systems," Teubner writes—just as the law has listened to both the educational system (cognitive ethology, zoology) and the economic system (factory farming) quite differently in the case of nonhuman animals—"but they do not give up their own requirement of agency."[11]

Still, as he notes, whenever the law grants new rights and duties, whenever it gives "associations between humans and non-humans a legal voice," the law opens itself to the ecology of its broader environment and the changes taking place there.[12] In the systems theory model, then, we have a picture of the legal system as both open *and* closed: open to its environment but responding to changes in it in terms of the autopoietic closure of its own self-reference. Such a model gives us, in fact, a more nuanced and complex way to explain what we examined at the outset in Hannah Arendt's work: the relationship between "rights" (and its ad hoc, ungrounded attribution) and the "right to have rights," a set of ontological or phenomenological attributes that falls outside the juridico-political as part of its environment and serves as a provocation or perturbation to the system itself. "The result of all this," Teubner concludes, "is that indeed non-humans gain access to social communication, albeit in a rather indirect way."[13]

From a systems theory point of view, the law may thus be seen as serving an "immunitary" function for society, as Esposito himself has emphasized. Indeed, he notes that Luhmann's thesis "that systems function not by rejecting conflicts and contradictions, but by producing them as necessary antigens for reactivating their own antibodies" places "the entire Luhmannian discourse within the semantic orbit of immunity."[14] As Luhmann explains in *Social Systems*, the code legal/illegal that steers the legal system "is supplemented by a binary coding of permitted/forbidden. This too serves to increase contradiction and to direct immune events in a precise way. . . . It helps to separate law from morality, setting law free to steer itself."[15] Crucially, this self-reference of the law's autopoeisis protects the communicative actions that take place in the legal domain from being steered or recoded by the moral distinction of "right vs. wrong"—a danger, I would add, that is dramatized daily in what is called the "public sphere" in the United States. Indeed, as Teubner notes, for a German intellectual of Luhmann's generation, that danger, and more broadly the "specifically German experience with mysticism and religiosity in the public sphere," is particularly resonant.[16] In Luhmann's account, the problem is that the moral code, under functional differentiation, "has detached itself," as William Rasch writes, "from its premodern locus in religion and has become a self-replicating, parasitic invader of the various modern, functionally differentiated social systems. . . . The danger comes, according to Luhmann, when the moral code—good/bad—attaches itself 'isomorphically,' one might say, to the prevailing codes of the respective function systems," so that what counts as knowledge in the education system, for example, gets recoded as morally "good" or morally "bad."[17] And "the effects Luhmann fears," as Rasch points out, "can be elucidated historically by listing the countless crusades, wars, inquisitions, and persecutions that moral discourse has fueled."[18]

For Luhmann as for Derrida, then, we find a permanent disjunction between ethics and law, or "justice" and "law" in Derrida's terms, and for both, it is a good thing, too. For both, the law is radically aporetic or paradoxical in its self-reference and immanence; the difference between legal and illegal is (paradoxically) itself instantiated by the legal, hence the tautological self-reference, "legal is legal." Or as Derrida puts it in "Force of Law," since "the foundation or ground, the position of the law can't by definition rest on anything but themselves, they are themselves a violence without ground. Which is not to say that they are in themselves unjust, in the sense of 'illegal.' They are neither legal nor illegal in their founding moment. They exceed the opposition between founded and unfounded."[19] In fact, they are constituted by what Derrida calls a *coup de force.*[20]

More technically speaking, the law is aporetic and without ground because of its "conditional" and "performative" character that simultaneously opens and propels it toward futurity by means of that which it has, in its contingent decisions, already excluded and, as it were, pushed to the position of the "next" or the "not yet fully addressed." Derrida articulates the problem quite precisely in "Force of Law":

> An address is always singular, idiomatic, and justice, as law (*droit*), seems always to suppose the generality of a rule, a norm or a universal imperative. How are we to reconcile the act of justice that must always concern singularity, individuals, irreplaceable groups and lives, the other or myself *as* other, in a unique situation, with rule, norm, value or the imperative of justice which necessarily have a general form, even if this generality prescribes a singular application in each case?[21]

Derrida's argument is not only that each "pragmatic instance" and iteration of the difference between law and justice must be attended to, but that indeed it is only in and through such iterative instances, and not in some transcendental ether, that law itself exists.[22] As Richard Beardsworth sums it up, "the law is, on the one hand, unaccountable," but "on the other hand it is *nowhere* but *in* its inscriptions in history, whilst not being reducible *to* these inscriptions either."[23] And this means that law is both unconditional *and* conditioned; it is the difference-as-iterability of the unconditional and conditioned.

Law and justice thus cannot be understood to be in a relationship of *opposition*, exactly, and in fact, as Martin Hägglund suggests, it is more useful to understand theirs as an "autoimmune" relation.[24] From this vantage, we might say that the problem with Esposito's Simondonian/Deleuzean tack at the end of *Bíos* is that it deals with only the first component of the aporia, only with what Derrida will call "unconditional hospitality," and not with the "after," the "conditional" character of law. It ignores, in other words, the fundamentally "autoimmunitary" character of the law—autoimmunitary not in the sense of "bad" or "negative" but in the sense of what I have elsewhere called the "openness from closure" principle, the fact that the inescapable self-referential closure of law is precisely, in its contingency, what opens it to the future and the outside, the as yet unaddressed subjects—who knows how many?—of justice.[25] As Derrida puts it in the interview "Autoimmunity: Real and Symbolic Suicides" (and this, explicitly in the context of a critique of the liberal pluralist—but also finally Christian—concept of "tolerance"), "pure and unconditional hospitality, hospitality *itself*, opens or is in advance open to someone who is neither expected nor invited, to whomever arrives as an absolutely foreign *visitor*, as a new *arrival*, nonidentifiable and unforeseeable, in short, wholly other."[26] On the other hand—and this is what gets overleapt in Esposito's conjugation of the radical equality of all "life" and the "norm" at the end of *Bíos*— "suspending or suppressing the immunity that protects me from the other might be nothing short of life-threatening," and so "an unconditional hospitality is, to be sure, practically impossible to live; one cannot in any case, and by definition, organize it." Thus, Derrida concludes, "this concept of pure hospitality can have no legal or political status," but at the same time, without it we would not "be able to determine any rules for conditional hospitality (with its rituals, its legal status, its norms, its national or international conventions)."[27]

In this sense, "Unconditional hospitality, which is neither juridical nor political, is nonetheless the condition of the political and the juridical."[28] But like justice, it can only take place in and through specific, pragmatic instances of iteration—instances that are by definition selective, exclusionary, and therefore "conditional." "I cannot expose myself to the coming of the other and offer him or her anything whatsoever," Derrida reminds us, "without making this hospitality effective, without, in some concrete way, giving *something determinate*. This determination will thus have to re-inscribe the unconditional into certain conditions. . . . Political, juridical, and ethical responsibilities have their place, if they take place, only in this transaction—which is each time unique, like an event—between these two hospitalities, the unconditional and the conditional."[29] In this light, if we want to salvage the Deleuzean impulse of Esposito's conjugation of life and norm—do we extend "unconditional hospitality" to anthrax and ebola virus, to SARS?—then we are necessarily driven back on a pragmatist rather than ontological reading of Deleuze (a point I've taken up in some detail elsewhere).[30] When I say "pragmatist" here I have in mind not the Rortyan variety but rather the sense that Derrida sounds in "Force of Law": not to "remain enclosed in purely speculative, theoretical, academic discourses but rather . . . to aspire to something more consequential, to *change* things."[31] By a pragmatist account, philosophy for Deleuze, as Paul Patton puts it, "is the invention or creation of concepts, the purpose of which is not accurate representation" but rather to provide "a form of description which is immediately practical," one "oriented toward the possibility of change."[32] Like Derrida's "beyond" and the "to come" which is not to be thought as a kind of Kantian regulative idea[33] but rather has the form of a promise, Deleuze and Guattari's "absolute deterritorialisation takes place in the virtual—as opposed to the actual—order of things," and "remains an unrealisable or impossible figure, manifest only in and through relative deterritorialisation."[34] On this reading, deterritorialisation obeys the logic of Derrida's iterability in and through which the "conditioned" and "unconditioned" are conjugated.[35] As Patton notes, Deleuze and Guattari "do not dwell on the aporetic character of the extreme or unconditioned form of the concepts outlined in *A Thousand Plateaus*" such as becoming, deterritorialization, and so on, but their essentially paradoxical and aporetic character is nonetheless clear.[36] All of which is made more difficult to see, in both Deleuze *and* Derrida, by an unfortunate reliance on terms such as "pure," "absolute," "authentic," "genuine," and so on.

The exercise of justice, then, while it would seem to require a kind of autonomy, indeed sovereignty, something on "the order of the 'I can,' ipseity,"[37] is in fact dependent on the pragmatic iteration of law, which is itself structured by the complex paradoxical relationship between "autonomy" and "automaticity" in Derrida's thought (a point I'll return to in some detail in a moment). As Derrida puts it in *Rogues*, if the event of justice "is to arrive or happen, it must, beyond all mastery, affect a passivity. It must touch an exposed vulnerability, one without absolute immunity, without indemnity. . . . In this regard, autoimmunity is not an absolute ill or evil. It enables exposure to the other, to *what* and to *who* comes—which means it must remain incalculable."[38] Here, we reach a key nexus in Derrida's thought regarding the performative, sovereignty, the immunitary, and the theological. As he writes in "Faith and Knowledge"—and in direct opposition to Carl Schmitt's attempt to severely limit the political[39]—"Religion and reason develop in tandem, drawing from this common resource: the testimonial pledge of the performative. . . . The same unique source divides itself mechanically, automatically, and sets itself reactively in opposition to itself: whence the two sources in one. This reactivity is a process of *sacrificial indemnification*, it strives to restore the unscathed (*helig*) that it itself threatens."[40]

As Derrida suggests in his rather remarkable discussion in *The Beast and the Sovereign*, we find this process at work in the very paradigm of the "ipseity" that characterizes the sovereign subject on the terrain of *both* the religious and the political: the phallus. Reaching all the way back to the worship of "fecundity or the generative potency of the Dionysiac mysteries," what is most striking here is "the *colossal automaticity* of the erection." On the one hand, it is "the maximum of life to be kept unscathed, indemnified, immune and safe," but on the other hand, "and precisely by virtue of its reflex-character," it is "that which is most mechanical, most separable from the life it represents."[41] The phallus is then both the very figure of sovereignty, ipseity, and at the same time "automatic, independent of will and even of desire," "mechanical, already in itself prosthetic." "Is it proper to man," he asks, "or else, already cut from man, is it a 'something,' a thing, an a-human, inhuman *what*, which is, moreover scarcely more masculine than feminine? Neither animal nor human?"[42] It is against this "con-fusion," we might say—against the fact that the phallus is, indeed, *bêtise*[43]—that the regime of sacrifice institutes itself, to reassert ipseity against automaticity, but only, fatefully, to performatively reiterate the very problem it attempts to solve. For as Hägglund notes in his discussion of Derrida's engagement of Schmitt, "the structure of decision undercuts . . . the possibility of an indivisible sovereignty." If the sovereign is to meet Schmitt's requirements of indivisibility and authority, then "he has to know who his enemy is and who he himself is in relation to his enemy." But if there is such knowledge, then there is no—can be no need for—the sovereign decision, which *is* a decision only insofar is there is no such knowledge. This means not only that sovereignty is subject to the "law of law" qua the performative; it also means that "there has *never* been an autonomous domain for the political."[44]

At stake here, then, is sovereignty in several different registers— not just of the nation-state but of the family, the familiar, the domestic, the "proper" to man, the *oikos* of the ecological, the economic, the *ethos* and the place of dwelling, of that which is "ours" or "mine" and deserves immunitary protection.[45] All of these are iterations of the "ipseity" of the autonomous subject (and the "auto-" of the "autobiographical animal"), whose very paradigm is the "head" of State.[46] It is worth recalling in this connection Derrida's discussion of the "*sacrificial* structure" of "carnophallogocentrism" in "Eating Well"[47] and his apparently (but only apparently) playful question there: "in our countries, who would stand any chance of becoming a *chef d'Etat* (a head of State), and of thereby acceding 'to the head,' by publicly, and therefore exemplarily, declaring him- or herself to be a vegetarian?"[48] The "ipseity" of sovereignty, in other words, requires not just "sacrificial indemnification" in some abstract sense but "carnivorous sacrifice" as testament to its autonomy, its phallic "freestandingness," you might say.[49]

Derrida's apparently playful analysis is even more resonant, I think, against the backdrop of the contemporary development known as synthetic or in vitro meat. Research into synthetic meat began in the late 1990s, and in 2008 the animal rights group PETA announced that it would award a $1 million prize to anyone who designed a process for commercially viable in vitro meat production by 2012.[50] The process is relatively new and involves variations, but typically scientists place myoblast cells from an animal in a nutrient medium where they multiply and then attach themselves to a scaffolding structure made of collagen or a similar substance. From there, the tissue continues to grow in a bioreactor until it reaches sufficient scale. The primary challenge of the technology is that the tissue grows in thin sheets, so achieving the proper three-dimensional density and texture of steak is presently impossible. The most likely commercial applications in the short run will therefore be in ground and processed foods. But the potential benefits of the technology, even beyond the signal virtue of reducing massive amounts of animal suffering, are enormous. Synthetic meat would no doubt reduce the incidence of epidemic zoonoses (such as "mad cow disease") because it could be engineered under much more controlled conditions than are possible in traditional livestock production, let alone the antibiotic-saturated practice of factory farming. And in terms of environmental impact, world meat production contributes to between 15 and 24 percent of total greenhouse gases (more than all cars, trains, planes, and ships combined), and it is water-, grain-, and energy-intensive to sustain—all of which is made even more pressing by the fact that total worldwide meat consumption is forecast to be 72 percent higher in 2030 than in 2000.[51]

Even without Derrida's anatomy of carnophallogocentrism, the example of synthetic meat makes palpable (if the expression may be allowed in this context) the value of a biopolitical framework for addressing these kinds of issues. From the point of view of, say, Peter Singer's utilitarian argument for animal rights on the basis of their fundamental interest in avoiding suffering, or Martha Nussbaum's argument for animal welfare from the standpoint of protecting their ability to "flourish," there *is* no ethical problem with synthetic meat.[52] But within the framework of biopolitics—particularly with an emphasis on its constitutive *dispositifs* such as we find in Foucault—the ethical and even political issues around synthetic meat take on a different cast. From this vantage, synthetic meat might not even appear to be an "animal" issue per se, and would instead be seen as utterly continuous with the technologies and *dispositifs* that are exercising a more and more finely tuned control over life and "making live" at the most capillary levels of social existence. Indeed, it would seem continuous with the practices of domestication, manipulation, and control of life that characterize the factory farms to which, from an animal rights point of view, it seems opposed.

It is all the more significant in this regard that current research in synthetic meat involves teams whose primary research has often been in fields of biomedicine such as vascular biology, regenerative medicine, and tissue engineering for human patients.[53] Given his remarks earlier on cloning, there is little doubt that Derrida would direct our attention, as Foucault's casting of biopolitics would as well, to the fundamentally mixed and ambivalent quality of these developments. But what Derrida's particular contribution to biopolitical thought helps us to plumb even more deeply are questions barred not just to the animal rights line of argument in support of synthetic meat but also to Esposito's invocation of "life" and even to Foucault's historical approach to *dispositifs*. He would push us to ask, is synthetic meat "life?" Would many of us feel that "real" meat is "better," more authentic, than synthetic meat because it indexes the sovereignty and ipseity of a subject who engages in sacrifice? Does sacrifice make meat taste better? Indeed, is it what makes meat "meat?" In light of Derrida's analysis of the alienating and "expropriative" effects of technoscience and how we respond to it—in the name of religion, in the name of "blood and soil"[54]—would eating synthetic meat be "eating well" in Derrida's sense? And why, indeed, would we otherwise ever think that eating meat had anything at all to do with patriotism and sovereignty, with the *"chef d'Etat"*?[55]

In this light, we can perhaps tease out an important deep structure of the locavore/"ethical carnivore" phenomenon: the fact that its followers "do not sacrifice sacrifice," as Derrida puts it in "Eating Well."[56] It enables us to explain the otherwise odd fact, as an essayist for the *Atlantic* notes, that many of the most prominent advocates of sustainable agriculture actually *oppose* synthetic meat. As one, a representative for the group Friends of the Earth, puts it, "At a time when hundreds of small-scale, sustainable farming operations are filing for bankruptcy every day, it is unethical to consider purchasing Petri dish

Sacrifice

meat." Another, speaking for the group Slow Food USA, suggests that cruelty to food animals is created primarily by the very growing gap between producers and consumers, a gap that is only widened by synthetic meat: "This is a technology that's just going to give more to companies and create a larger distance between us."[57] Against the alienating and derealizing mechanicity of "tele-technoscientific capitalism," we find here, in Derrida's words, if not a "fundamentalism," then an "integrism" of "blood and soil" that drives us back to "the family (*heimisch*, homely), to the familiar, to the domestic, to the proper, to the *oikos* of the ecological and of the economic, to the *ethos*, to the place of dwelling," only to reenact the "auto-immune auto-indemnification" that results from the sacrificial closure and securing of the "proper."[58] After all, why eat animals *at all*? We have to account here, then, for "a double postulation: *on the one hand*, the absolute respect of life, the 'Thou shalt not kill' (at least thy neighbour, if not the living in general), the 'fundamentalist' prohibition of abortion, of artificial insemination, of performative intervention in the genetic potential, even to the ends of gene therapy, etc.; *and on the other* . . . the no less universal sacrificial vocation."[59]

When we ask what "the *mechanics* of this double postulation" are, as Derrida puts it, we find an "apparently very simple" but disarming principle which we will have already guessed from Derrida's analysis of the phallus: "life has absolute value only if it is worth *more than* life. . . . It is sacred, holy, infinitely respectable only in the name of what is worth more than it and what is not restricted to the naturalness of the bio-zoological (sacrificeable). . . . Thus, respect of life in the discourses of religion as such concerns 'human life' only in so far as it bears witness, in some manner, to the infinite transcendence of that which is worth more than it (divinity, the sacrosanctness of the law)."[60] And here, we should recall, with Esposito, perhaps the most brazen manifestation of this logic in the history of the modern political (or is it theological?) stage: Hitler, in telegram number 71 sent from his bunker in Berlin as the Allies were approaching, ordered that all means of subsistence for the German people, who had shown themselves unworthy of the Reich, should be destroyed. "Here the limit point of the Nazi antinomy becomes suddenly clear," Esposito writes; "the life of some, and finally the life of one, is sanctioned only by the death of everyone."[61] Against this multiply inflected background, it is all the more suggestive, I think, that the leading figure in the scientific push toward synthetic meat, eighty-seven-year-old Willem van Eelen—who in 1999 was granted the first US and international patents for the "Industrial Production of Meat Using Cell Culture Methods"—spent most of World War II in prison camps, where the similarities between how prisoners and animals were treated left an indelible impression on him, fueling what he later discovered as his life's work.[62] Were we to put Derrida's words in his mouth, he might well say: "no more sacrificial indemnification!"

Here, it seems to me, we find an advance beyond Luhmann's functionalist analysis of the "immunitary" logic of the law. As Gunther Teubner observes, "It is this transcendence of positivity wherein Jacques Derrida's contribution lies."[63] As he notes, for systems theory,

> secularization is supposed to be a de-transcendentalization of all social subsystems and a concentration on transcendence in only one system of meaning, that of religion. But is this not at variance with the tough resistance to secularization of social utopias (socialism, fascism, neo-liberal doctrines of salvation), palpable even, and especially, in the highly rationalized subsystems of politics, law, the economy or science? Is there not an otherwise inexplicable manifestation here of salvific doctrines, eschatological hopes?[64]

Indeed, speaking in the context of the contemporary "wars of religion" that occupy so much of the discussion in *Philosophy in a Time of Terror*, Derrida writes in "Faith and Knowledge" that "The fundamental concepts that often permit us to isolate or to *pretend* to isolate the *political*—restricting ourselves to this particular circumscription—remain religious or any case theologico-political."[65] This does not mean that Derrida becomes late in his career a "philosopher of religion," nor is it to suggest that there is a fundamental "religious turn" during that same period. It is simply to say that both religion and politics are constituted by the same logic of "autoimmune auto-indemnification," and for that very reason they inflect and "infect" each other.[66]

From this vantage, we can appreciate more readily the deeply imbricated relationship between globalization (or *mondialisation*, as

Derrida prefers to say) and the "globalatinization" Derrida takes up in "Faith and Knowledge,"[67] a process that involves "this strange alliance of Christianity, as the experience of the death of God, and tele-technoscientific capitalism,"[68] a "return of the religious" (both Christian and Muslim)[69] at the very same moment of the most extreme "expropriative and delocalizing" effects of capitalism and its constitutive technologies.[70] As Derrida writes in *Rogues*, this globalization is "more inegalitarian and violent than ever," confiscating and concentrating wealth and natural resources with enormous force and efficiency and reserving "for that small part of the world those two great forms of immunity that go by the names of public health and military security."[71] This process presents itself—justifies itself—as a peacekeeping or "*pacifying*" gesture that, in the name of prosperity, disguises a war "without limit" against "the religious cultures, states, nations or ethnic groups they represent" in the name of access "that is immediate and potentially without limit, to the same world market."[72] What this means, as Leonard Lawlor observes, is that for Derrida "*globalization is war 'by other means.'* Even more, the violence of this war, which is violence against the living in general, is autoimmune precisely because it is global and therefore limitless."[73]

The explicitly biopolitical character of this fact—and its obvious resonances with Foucault's work—are clear in *Philosophy in a Time of Terror*, where Derrida asks, "does terrorism have to work only through death? Can't one terrorize without killing? And does killing necessarily mean putting to death? Isn't it also 'letting die'? Can't 'letting die,' 'not wanting to know that one is letting others die'—hundreds of millions of human beings, from hunger, AIDS, lack of medical treatment, and so on—also be part of a 'more or less' conscious and deliberate terrorist strategy?"[74] Here, it seems to me, what needs to be added to Derrida's analysis of "not wanting to know" is an element not precluded by it but not exactly amplified by it either: the specific role and character of industrially produced meat as a central element and tool in the biopolitical process of globalatinization, in which we find the "prosperity" and "well-being" of the subject-consumer channeled through not just the consumerist "choice" that capitalist globalization says it offers and on which it depends, but also through the complex psychodynamics of sacrifice and eating flesh as a sign of

perfect

the subject's autonomy, security, and "indemnification," "an ipseity that includes within itself, as the etymology would also confirm, the androcentric positioning of power in the master or head of the household, the sovereign mastery of the lord or seigneur, of the father or husband."[75] In other words, "carnophallogocentrism" is a key export for the success of capitalist globalization, one borne on the backs of billions of dead animals.

Take China, for example—a country known for thousands of years for its predilection for vegetables over meat—where per capita intake of poultry, pork, fish, and meat has more than tripled since 1970. As a recent article notes, "in nearly every country where meat consumption was low (even in countries such as China, where some Buddhist practices encouraged vegetarianism), per capita intake has paralleled economic development."[76] And because of the scale of the Chinese population, the extreme inefficiency of meat as a food source (it takes 40 kilograms of feed to produce 1 kilogram of beef), and the scarcity of farmland in China, "China's meat mania is implicated in everything from deforestation in Brazil to food-price inflation in Africa."[77] Here, in the name of "prosperity" and "public health" (as Derrida puts it) we find a massive "not wanting to know," but a "not wanting to know" of a rather specific sort: not just "not wanting to know" that nonhuman animals are being put to death on a new and unprecedented scale, but also a not wanting to know that the very ecological sustainability of the planet is at stake in the repression of this violence against nonhuman animals. For as Paul Roberts notes, over the next forty years, worldwide meat consumption is expected to more than double current levels, as cheap, industrially produced meat follows in the wake of capitalist development under globalization. And yet it is far from clear that the planet can support, let alone sustain, the ecological fallout of this newly exported sign of "prosperity." As he puts it, "In a strange way, such bleak forecasts bring a welcome clarity to a discussion long confined to the margins of society. . . . Now the idea that meat-eating is purely an individual choice, and the costs affect only the individual, has been blown wide open." Thus, he argues, eating meat has "graduated from the category of lifestyle choice to that of collective responsibility."[78]

By way of moving toward a conclusion, then, we can mark a series of advances, I think, in deepening and broadening our understanding of the place of nonhuman animals and our relations to them in a biopolitical frame—or rather, *places*, given how multiple and conflicted that status is: from the crucial move in Agamben that insists on not just one set of terms but two—not just "human/animal" but also *bios/zoe* in shifting transposition within and across species lines; to the finally excessive formalism of his rendering of the biopolitical symmetry between the sovereign and *homo sacer*; to the Foucauldian shift toward the constitutive *dispositifs* of biopolitics that cut across species lines and knit together bodies of whatever kind; to Esposito's analysis of the crucial function of race (and therefore, I have been arguing, species) and his framing of the immunitary logic of biopolitics; and finally to Derrida's anatomy of "auto-immune auto-indemnification."[79] For Agamben, the relationship between the growth and export of industrially produced meat to capitalist globalization would not be political, much less biopolitical, at all; for Foucault, it would be biopolitical in the sense of being continuous with the radical ambivalence attendant on the ever-increasing rationalization and control of "life" as a political and economic resource, of "making live" and "letting die," that is constitutive of the biopolitical in its modern form; and it would be, moreover, potentially integral to a "new schema of politicization";[80] for Esposito, the emphasis on its biopolitical character would surely fall not just on the fact that here we find that "the body that experiences ever more intensely the indistinction between power and life is no longer that of the individual, nor is it that sovereign body of nations, but that body of the world that is both torn and unified,"[81] but also on the fact of an immunitary mechanism that would allow us to explain the differences between how the Nazis treated their pets, their meat, and their Holocaust victims. What Derrida adds to this already impressive list of advances is not just his anatomy of the fundamental psychic and cultural mechanisms that are crucial to the biopolitical regimes of the (auto)immunitary and the "sacrificial" via the essential "carnophallogocentrism" of sovereignty in both the political and theological registers—the matrix in which the "auto-" of "man" as the "autobiographical animal," the "autoimmune," "autonomy," and "automaticity" reside—but also the *direct* address he gives, alone in this group, to (at least some—who knows how many?)

nonhuman animals as potential subjects of justice, as those to whom the "thou shalt not kill" of immunitary protection might apply.

Here, then, the biopolitical finds a new vocation, precisely by sustaining and deepening the logic that already constitutes it—a logic that, if pushed far enough, breaks down the stark opposition between the thanatopolitical and the affirmative that has tended to paralyze biopolitical thought: *either* unconditionally embrace all forms of life as subjects of immunitary protection, *or* suffer the autoimmune consequences that follow. But what this either/or logic misses is that the performative structure and logic of immunitary indemnification is precisely the condition of possibility for any possible affirmation, thus opening the community to its others—potentially, *all* its others, wherein reside the inseparable possibilities of both promise and threat. Hospitality, *to be* hospitality, to be real, must be something "determinate" and "conditioned"; my laws will not protect you if they aren't. But this act of selection and discrimination, in its contingency and finitude, is precisely what opens it to the other and to the future. This is why discrimination, selection, self-reference, and exclusion cannot be avoided, and it is also why the refusal to take seriously the differences between different forms of life—bonobos versus sunflowers, let's say—as subjects of immunitary protection is, as they used to say in the 1970s, a "cop out." This very act of immunitary selection and protection on the basis of the capacity to "respond"—a capacity itself based on a constitutively prosthetic relation to technicity—can never be juridical, however, because it is always already traced with the automaticity and mechanicity of a reaction. It is a "line," to use Derrida's formulation, that is always already "multiple" and nonlinear, always folded and in motion, always under erasure. We *must* choose, and by definition we *cannot* choose everyone and everything at once. But this is precisely what ensures that, *in* the future, we *will have been wrong.* Our "determinate" act of justice now will have been shown to be *too* determinate, revealed to have left someone or something out. Indeed, this is precisely what has unfolded over the past few decades regarding our rapidly changing understanding of nonhuman animals and how we relate to them. *All* of them? How many? Who knows? These are not rhetorical questions. But I have suggested in the foregoing at least a place to start, since all cannot be welcomed, nor all at once.

As Derrida notes in "Autoimmunity: Real and Symbolic Suicides," we are thus always returned to a fundamental aporia that we must confront in two registers. Logically, "the demos is *at once* the incalculable singularity of anyone, before any 'subject,' . . . beyond all citizenship, beyond every 'state,' indeed every 'people,' indeed even beyond the current state of the definition of a living being as living 'human being,' *and* the universality of rational calculation, of the equality of citizens before the law."[82]

In the end, then—to return to where we began—the biopolitical frame has the virtue of recasting our current legal and political norms to enable us to see the irony (if one wants to call it that) of the Spanish Parliament's decision with regard to human rights for Great Apes at the very moment when the violence of biopolitics against "the body of the world" has never been more virulent and more systematic, nowhere more so than in today's practices of factory farming. Nor has it been less concerned with the distinctions in taxonomy between human and nonhuman life with regard to "making live" and "letting die." So even as granting basic rights to Great Apes—or indeed to other nonhuman animals as well—no doubt constitutes a monumental and historic step forward for our relations with animals within the political purview of liberal democracy and its legal framework, it might well be seen, within the biopolitical context opened up by Foucault, Esposito, Derrida, and others, as essentially a kind of tokenism in which nonhumans who are "racially" similar enough to us to achieve recognition are protected, while all around us a Holocaust—if that is indeed the word we want—against our other fellow creatures rages on and indeed accelerates. An affirmative biopolitics need not—indeed, as I have argued, *cannot*—simply embrace "life" in all its undifferentiated singularity, even as Esposito is surely right that confronting "the biojuridical node between life and norm" is "neither the content nor the final sense of biopolitics, but is at a minimum its presupposition."[83] What is useful about biopolitical thought is that it puts us in a position to articulate the disjunctive and uneven quality of our own political moment, constituted as it is by new forces and new actors not very legible by the political vocabulary of sovereignty we have inherited, enabling us to see not just the dramatic, affirmative shift announced by the Spanish Parliament's decision, but also the radically ambivalent character of the biopolitical: that that decision is shadowed, indeed haunted, by the mechanized killing of billions of animals each year, in factory farming, in aquaculture, in the fishing of the seas to the point of collapse, in the sixth largest extinction event in the history of the planet that we are now experiencing—what Jonathan Safran Foer rightly calls a "war" on our fellow creatures.[84] The biopolitical point is no longer "human" vs. "animal"; the biopolitical point is a newly expanded community of the living and the concern we should all have with where violence and immunitary protection fall within it, because we are all, after all, potentially animals before the law.

Notes

SECTION ONE

1. Martin Heidegger, "The Question Concerning Technology," trans. William Lovitt, in Heidegger, *Basic Writings*, ed. and intro. David Farrell Krell (New York: Harper and Row, 1977), 302.

2. Ibid., 287, 294.

3. As David Wills aptly summarizes it, *Gestell* "is coined in the context of two other words, namely *Gebirge*, the gathering of mountains that produces the mountain 'range,' and *Gemut*, the gathering of emotions that produces a 'disposition.' In comparison with a natural gathering on the one hand and human gathering on the other, *Gestell* will be the frameworking of what is set out, produced by and in the same movement ordered into instrumental service." David Wills, *Dorsality: Thinking Back through Technology and Politics* (Minneapolis: University of Minnesota Press, 2008), 30.

4. Heidegger, "The Question Concerning Technology," 309.

5. Ibid., 308.

6. Ibid.

7. Ibid., 299.

8. Ibid., 310.

9. Ibid., 300.

10. Ibid., 294.

11. For as Timothy Campbell points out, the decisive question here is this: "What kind of man masters technology? The change in the species of man that attempts to extend his domination over technology . . . is in fact what is most dangerous about technology." Timothy Campbell, *Improper Life: Technology and Biopolitics from Heidegger to Agamben* (Minneapolis: University of Minnesota Press, 2011), 7.

12. Martin Heidegger, "Letter on Humanism," trans. Frank A. Capuzzi and J. Glenn Gray, in Heidegger, *Basic Writings*, 200.

13. See Cary Wolfe, *Animal Rites: American Culture, the Discourse of Species, and Posthumanist Theory,* foreword W. J. T. Mitchell (Chicago: University of Chicago Press, 2008), chap. 2. As Heidegger puts it in the "Letter," "man is not only a

living creature who possesses language along with other capacities. Rather, language is the house of Being in which man ek-sists by dwelling, in that he belongs to the truth of Being, guarding it." Heidegger, "Letter on Humanism," 213.

14. Campbell, *Improper Life*, 28.

15. Throughout this essay, I roughly alternate between the more technically correct term "nonhuman animal" and the more concise and felicitous term "animal," it being obvious that *Homo sapiens* is but one member of the animal kingdom—and a member who has often sought to maintain that the "human" is not.

16. For Derrida's discussion of "ipseity," see Jacques Derrida, *Rogues: Two Essays on Reason*, trans. Pascale-Anne Brault and Michael Naas (Stanford, CA: Stanford University Press, 2005), 143, and Jacques Derrida, *The Beast and the Sovereign*, ed. Michel Lisse, Marie-Louise Mallet, and Ginette Michaud, trans. Geoffrey Bennington, vol. 1 (Chicago: University of Chicago Press, 2009), 71. The canonical locus for the discussion of "bare life" in Agamben is his *Homo Sacer: Sovereign Power and Bare Life*, trans. Daniel Heller-Roazen (Stanford, CA: Stanford University Press, 1998).

17. See Jacques Derrida, "*Geschlecht* II: Heidegger's Hand," trans. John P. Leavey Jr., in *Deconstruction and Philosophy*, ed. John Sallis (Chicago: University of Chicago Press, 1986), 173.

18. Jacques Derrida, "The Parergon," trans. Craig Owens, *October* 9 (Summer 1979): 33. As Wills notes, *Gestell* is a kind of technology through which the human paradoxically reveals its essential, pretechnological, ontological nature to itself only on the basis of its prosthetic dependence on something external, technical, inorganic (Wills, *Dorsality*, 34).

19. See Roberto Esposito, *Immunitas: The Protection and Negation of Life* (London: Polity Press, 2011), 7.

20. Hannah Arendt, *The Human Condition*, 2nd ed., intro. Margaret Conovan (Chicago: University of Chicago Press, 1998), 2.

21. Hannah Arendt, *The Origins of Totalitarianism*, new ed. (New York: Harcourt, 1976), 302.

22. Ibid., 292. For an incisive discussion of this moment in Arendt, see Alistair Hunt, "The Rights of the Infinite," in *Qui Parle* 19, no. 2 (Spring/Summer 2011): 223–51.

23. Jacques Derrida, *The Animal That Therefore I Am*, ed. Marie-Louise Mallet, trans. David Wills (New York: Fordham University Press, 2008), 30. See also Jacques Derrida, *Of Spirit: Heidegger and the Question*, trans. Geoffrey Bennington and Rachel Bowlby (Chicago: University of Chicago Press, 1989), 56. On "bare life," see Agamben, *Homo Sacer*.

24. Arendt, *Origins of Totalitarianism*, 295–96.

25. Ibid., 296–97.

26. As Arendt writes in her overview of the idea of politics inherited from the Greeks, in a passage whose direct lines of descent to Heidegger's humanism are

clear enough, and in one of the great articulations of the biopolitical distinction between *bios* and *zoe* before Foucault, "The distinction between man and animal runs
right through the human species itself: only the best (*aristoi*), who constantly prove
themselves to be the best (*aristeuein*, a verb for which there is no equivalent in any
other language) and who 'prefer immortal fame to mortal things,' are really human;
the others, content with whatever pleasures nature will yield them, live and die like
animals" (*The Human Condition*, 19; see also 13, 24, 37).

27. See in particular her discussion of what she calls, in quotation marks, the
"'language' of mathematical symbols" versus language proper, which partakes of
the *topos* we have already discussed in Heidegger of the improper versus proper use
relation to language as mere communication, information, in contrast to authentic
expression and comprehension (Arendt, *The Human Condition*, 3–4). See also her
Origins of Totalitarianism, 297.

28. Arendt, *The Human Condition*, 3; see also 27.

29. Arendt, *Origins of Totalitarianism*, 300.

30. See Jacques Derrida, "Structure, Sign, and Play in the Discourse of the Human Sciences," in *Margins of Philosophy*, trans. Alan Bass (Chicago: University of
Chicago Press, 1978), 278–94.

31. As she writes in the prologue to *The Human Condition*, "wherever the *relevance* of speech is at stake, matters become political by definition, for speech is what
makes man a political being" (Arendt, *The Human Condition*, 4; emphasis added).
So speech is "natural" but, regarding its function as a foundation for rights, it may
be *either* relevant or irrelevant. Indeed, as she notes in discussing Aristotle's political writings, "according to this opinion, everybody outside the *polis*—slaves and
barbarians—was *aneu logou*, deprived, of course, not of the faculty of speech, but
of *a way of life* in which speech and only speech made sense and where the central
concern of all citizens was to talk with each other" (ibid., 27; emphasis added). All
of the foregoing clarifies why Hunt is not quite right when he says of Arendt that
"insofar as the right to have rights is claimed by those reduced to a condition of
rightlessness, perhaps the author of *The Human Condition*, one of the most magnifi-
cent humanist treatises of the twentieth century, is in her own way also an advocate
of animal rights" (Hunt, "The Rights of the Infinite," 225). The right to have rights
would be barred to nonhuman animals because it rests on the foundation of the
capacity for speech.

32. Derrida, *The Animal That Therefore I Am*, 27–29.

33. "If it belonged to everyone," Esposito continues, "like a biological characteristic, language or the ability to walk, for example, a right would not be a right, but
simply a fact with no need for specific juridical denomination. In the same way, if the
category of person coincided with that of human being, there would have been no
need for it. Ever since its original juridical performance, personhood is valuable exactly to the extent to which it is not applicable to all, and finds its meaning precisely
in the principled difference between those to whom it is, from time to time, attributed

and those to whom it is not, or from whom, at a certain point, it is subtracted. Only if there are men (and women) who are not completely, or not at all, considered persons, can others be or become such." Roberto Esposito, "The Person and Human Life," trans. Diana Garvin and Thomas Kelso, in *Theory after "Theory,"* ed. Jane Elliott and Derek Attridge (London: Routledge, 2011), 209.

34. "'Eating Well,' or the Calculation of the Subject: An Interview with Jacques Derrida," trans. Peter Connor and Avital Ronnell, in *Who Comes After the Subject?* ed. Eduardo Cadava, Peter Connor, and Jean-Luc Nancy (New York: Routledge, 1991), 112. It is worth voicing a clarification here with regard to "sacrifice." Sacrifice in Agamben would appear to be *opposed* to, not a part of, Derrida's "sacrificial symbolic economy" when Agamben asserts that *homo sacer* "is a human victim who may be killed but not sacrificed" (*Homo Sacer*, 83). But what "sacrificed" references here for Agamben is, additionally, an earlier religious order out of which the properly political emerges, which is assimilated in Derrida's reading to the same essential logic. "The political sphere of sovereignty . . . takes the form of a zone of indistinction between sacrifice and homicide," Agamben writes (*Homo Sacer*, 83). In other words, *homo sacer* as he who may be "killed but not sacrificed" means, as it does in Derrida, "killable but not murderable" but retains in Agamben the earlier religious sense as well.

35. Derrida's title "Before the Law" is taken, it should be noted (while speaking of frames), from the short story by Franz Kafka of the same title, which itself appears as part of Kafka's longer text *The Trial*—and, moreover, as a text centrally engaged by Agamben in *Homo Sacer,* 49–57. Jacques Derrida, "Before the Law," trans. Avital Ronnell, in *Act of Literature,* ed. Derek Attridge (New York: Routledge, 1992), 193–94, 197–98.

36. It is, Derrida observes, "linked with the upright position, that is, to a certain *elevation.* The passage to the upright position raises man, thus distancing his nose from the sexual zones, anal or genital. This distance ennobles his height and leaves its traces by delaying his action. Delay, difference, ennobling elevation, diversion of the olfactory sense from the sexual stench, repression—here are the origins of morality" (Derrida, "Before the Law," 193). For a fuller discussion, see Wolfe, *Animal Rites*, chap. 3.

37. Derrida, "Before the Law," 193.

38. Ibid., 194.

39. Derrida, "Eating Well," 112, 114.

SECTION TWO

1. Paola Cavalieri and Peter Singer, eds., *The Great Ape Project: Equality beyond Humanity* (New York: St. Martin's Press, 1993), 4. A similar bill, The Great Ape Protection Act (HR 1326), focused on prohibiting invasive research and providing

for suitable retirement and care of great apes already used in research, was introduced in the US House of Representatives on April 17, 2008, and again on March 5, 2009, with a companion bill, S3694, reaching the US Senate on August 3, 2010.

2. United Poultry Concerns, "Average and Total Numbers of Animals Who Died to Feed Americans in 2008," last accessed July 19, 2011, http://www.upc-online.org/slaughter/2008americans.html.

3. *Putting Meat on the Table: Industrial Farm Animal Production in America: A Report of the Pew Commission on Industrial Farm Animal Production*, foreword John Carlin, preface Robert P. Martin, 38. Last accessed July 19, 2011, http://www.ncifap.org/bin/e/j/PCIFAPFin.pdf.

4. Erik Marcus, *Meat Market: Animals, Ethics, and Money* (Boston: Brio Press, 2005), 45–46.

5. See, e.g.,. Ibid., 46–47, and Jonathan Safran Foer, *Eating Animals* (New York: Little, Brown, 2009), 133–36.

6. Evelyn Thiess, "Should the USDA Make Dietary Guidelines While It Promotes the Meat and Dairy Industry?" *Cleveland Plain Dealer*, March 7, 2011. Last accessed July 19, 2011, http://www.cleveland.com/healthfit/index.ssf/2011/03/should_the_usda_make_dietary_g.html.

7. D. Smith, "Rats, Mice, and Birds Excluded from Animal Welfare Act," *American Psychological Association: Monitor on Psychology* 33, no. 7 (July 2002). Last accessed July 19, 2011, http://www.apa.org/monitor/julaug02/rats.aspx.

8. As it appears in sec. 2, item A of the original 1966 Animal Welfare Act.

9. See Steven M. Wise, *Rattling the Cage: Toward Legal Rights for Animals* (Cambridge, MA: Perseus Publishing, 2000), 4, 267–68.

10. Richard A. Epstein, "Animals as Objects, or Subjects, of Rights," in *Animal Rights: Current Debates and New Directions*, ed. Cass R. Sunstein and Martha C. Nussbaum (New York: Oxford University Press, 2004), 158.

11. Richard A. Posner, "Animal Rights: Legal, Philosophical, and Pragmatic Perspectives," in *Animal Rights: Current Debates and New Directions*, ed. Cass R. Sunstein and Martha C. Nussbaum (New York: Oxford University Press, 2004), 51.

12. Ibid., 57.

13. Epstein, "Animals as Objects," 55. See Cary Wolfe, *Animal Rites: American Culture, the Discourse of Species, and Posthumanist Theory* (Chicago: University of Chicago Press, 2003), chap. 1.

14. Posner, "Animal Rights," 58.

15. Though Peter Singer's *Animal Liberation* (New York: Avon Books, 1975) and Tom Regan's *The Case for Animal Rights* (Berkeley: University of California Press, 1983) are more well known—indeed, they are the founding philosophical texts of the animal rights movement—it is probably Paola Cavalieri's *The Animal Question: Why Nonhuman Animals Deserve Human Rights* (New York: Oxford University Press, 2001), that provides the most compelling argument, within analytic philosophy, for adapting the rights framework to (at least some) nonhuman animals.

16. Posner, "Animal Rights," 57–58.

17. Epstein, "Animals as Objects," 157. Tom Regan, "The Case for Animal Rights," in *In Defense of Animals*, ed. Peter Singer (New York: Harper and Row, 1985), 17.

18. Regan, "The Case for Animal Rights," 17. Singer zeroes in on Posner's contention that "I believe that ethical argument is and should be powerless against tenacious moral instincts" and offers his version of Regan's charge in the *Slate* reply: "If this supports our current treatment of animals, why should it not also be used to support other preferences for 'our own,' which appear to be just as much a brute fact about human beings as a preference for our own species? Here is one example: 'We must be honest, decent, loyal, and friendly to members of our blood and no one else. What happens to the Russians, what happens to the Czechs, is a matter of utter indifference to me.' The speaker is Heinrich Himmler. He goes on to say, 'Whether the other races live in comfort or perish of hunger interests me only insofar as we need them as slaves for our culture; apart from that it does not interest me.'" Peter Singer, "Ethics beyond Species and beyond Instincts: A Response to Richard Posner," in *Animal Rights: Current Debates and New Directions*, ed. Cass R. Sunstein and Martha C. Nussbaum (New York: Oxford University Press, 2004), 87.

19. Singer, "Ethics beyond Species," 87.

20. Posner, "Animal Rights," 59.

21. Epstein, "Animals as Objects," 156.

22. Posner, "Animal Rights," 59.

23. Singer, "Ethics beyond Species," 90.

24. For a brief overview, see James Rachels, "Drawing Lines," in *Animal Rights: Current Debates and New Directions*, ed. Cass R. Sunstein and Martha C. Nussbaum (New York: Oxford University Press, 2004), 162–63. For an excellent, detailed discussion of current law and enforcement as it pertains to factory farming, see, in that same collection, David J. Wolfson and Mariann Sullivan, "Foxes in the Hen House: Animals, Agribusiness, and the Law: A Modern American Fable," 205–33.

25. See Regan, *The Case for Animal Rights*, 174–85.

26. Joel Feinberg, "The Rights of Animals and Future Generations," in *Rights, Justice, and the Bounds of Liberty: Essays in Social Philosophy* (Princeton, NJ: Princeton University Press, 1980), 184. It is worth noting, however—in both Feinberg's discussion and in essays that examine his seminal work in a special issue of the journal *Legal Theory*—that the category of "the animal" is subject to the sort of generic flattening that Derrida warns us about in his criticism of the locution "*the* animal" (even though Feinberg himself does at least differentiate between what he calls "higher" from "lower" animals at the end of his essay). The problem in these discussions is not just that the category of "animals" is extraordinarily undifferentiated—as if bonobos, stingrays, and mosquitoes could be discussed in the same breath. It is also that the analogy between the interests of animals and those of hu-

man infants bears crucial weight in Feinberg's argument. As Christopher Heath Wellman points out, "Feinberg's case in favor of animal rights hinges upon a *reductio ad absurdum;* he argues that one cannot deny that animals can have rights unless one is similarly willing to deny that wee babies can have rights" (Christopher Heath Wellman, "Feinberg's Two Concepts of Rights," *Legal Theory* 11 [2005]: 219). But this ignores the obvious fact that at least some animals (i.e., at a minimum, ones Feinberg calls "higher") obviously have *greater* "conative urges" than human infants, and thus bear a greater range of interests.

27. Jacques Derrida and Elisabeth Roudinesco, *For What Tomorrow: A Dialogue,* trans. Jeff Fort (Stanford, CA: Stanford University Press, 2004), 64, 74. I have discussed the work of both Derrida and Diamond in greater detail elsewhere. See, e.g., my essay "Exposures," in Stanley Cavell, Cora Diamond, John McDowell, Ian Hacking, and Cary Wolfe, *Philosophy and Animal Life* (New York: Columbia University Press, 2008), 1–41.

28. Derrida and Roudinesco, *For What Tomorrow* , 65.

29. Ibid., 74.

30. Ibid. As Derrida observes, "In general, in the European philosophical tradition, there is no conception of a (finite) subject of law [*droit*] who is not a subject of duty (Kant sees only two exceptions to this law [*loi*]: God, whose rights are without duty, and slaves, who have duties but no rights). It is once again a matter of the inherited concepts of the subject, the political subject, the citizen, the sovereign self-determination of the subject of law . . ." (ibid.). On the French distinction between *droit* and *loi*, see. Ibid., 212 n. 19.

31. Cora Diamond, "The Difficulty of Reality and the Difficulty of Philosophy," in Stanley Cavell, Cora Diamond, John McDowell, Ian Hacking, and Cary Wolfe, *Philosophy and Animal Life* (New York: Columbia University Press, 2008), 74.

32. Cora Diamond, "Injustice and Animals," in *Slow Cures and Bad Philosophers: Essays on Wittgenstein, Medicine, and Bioethics,* ed. Carl Elliott (Durham, NC: Duke University Press, 2001), 121, 136.

33. Giorgio Agamben, *State of Exception,* trans. Kevin Attell (Chicago: University of Chicago Press, 2005), 1.

34. Judith Butler, *Precarious Life: The Powers of Mourning and Violence* (London: Verso, 2004), 26, 27.

35. Ibid., 30.

36. See, e.g., Marc Bekoff, *The Emotional Lives of Animals* (Novato, CA: New World Library, 2007).

37. "There Is a Person Here: An Interview with Judith Butler," in *International Journal of Sexuality and Gender Studies* 6, nos. 1/2 (2001): 16.

38. "Antigone's Claim: A Conversation with Judith Butler," in *Theory and Event* 12, no. 1 (2009): 7.

39. Judith Butler, *Frames of War: When Is Life Grievable?* (London: Verso, 2009), 18, 16.

40. Ibid., 19.

41. For an enlightening discussion of this topic, see Rebecca Skloot, "Creature Comforts," *New York Times Magazine* (Dec. 31, 2008). Last accessed July 19, 2011, http://www.nytimes.com/2009/01/04/magazine/04Creatures-t.html?scp=1&sq=service%20animals&st=cse.

42. I discuss this matter in some detail in "Exposures," esp. 21–34.

43. See, e.g., her refutation of the charge that "I may seem to be positing a new basis for humanism." This is not so, she argues, because "a vulnerability must be perceived and recognized in order to come into play in an ethical encounter," and "when a vulnerability *is* recognized, that recognition has the power to change the meaning and structure of the vulnerability itself." Hence "it follows that vulnerability is fundamentally dependent on existing norms of recognition if it is to be attributed to any human subject" (Butler, *Precarious Life*, 42–43). This exempts Butler from the Heideggerian humanism problem, but only to thrust on her the problem of a reciprocity model of ethics, as I am about to take it up.

44. Butler, *Precarious Life*, 44.

45. Ibid., 45.

46. Ibid., 31.

47. Or moral agents vs. moral patients, see Cavalieri, *Animal Question*, 29–30.

48. See my "Postmodern Ethics, the Question of the Animal, and the Imperatives of Posthumanist Theory," the conclusion to *Animal Rites*, esp. 194–99. The closest that Butler comes to this position is her contention that "*Whether or not we continue to enforce a universal conception of human rights at moments of outrage and incomprehension, precisely when we think that others have taken themselves out of the human community as we know it, is a test of our very humanity.* We make a mistake, therefore, if we take a single definition of the human, or a single model of rationality, to be the defining feature of the human" (*Precarious Life*, 89–90).

49. Butler, *Precarious Life*, 31.

50. Ibid., 91.

51. Ibid., 104.

52. Quoted in Roberto Esposito, *Bios: Biopolitics and Philosophy*, trans. and intro. Timothy Campbell (Minneapolis: University of Minnesota Press, 2008), 33.

53. Michel Foucault, *"Society Must Be Defended": Lectures at the Collège de France, 1975–1976*, ed. Mauro Bertani and Alessandro Fontana, trans. David Macey (New York: Picador, 2003), 247.

54. Ibid., 35–36.

55. Esposito, *Bios*, 29.

56. Michel Foucault, *The Birth of Biopolitics: Lectures at the Collège de France, 1978–1979*, ed. Michel Senellart, trans. Graham Burchell (New York: Palgrave Macmillan, 2008), 271–72.

57. Ibid., 272.

58. Ibid., 274.

59. Diamond, "Injustice and Animals." For a comprehensive discussion of Diamond's position, see Cary Wolfe, *What Is Posthumanism?* (Minneapolis: University of Minnesota Press, 2010), chap. 3.

60. Foucault, *The Birth of Biopolitics*, 271.

61. Ibid., 274.

62. Ibid., 282, 283.

63. Ibid., 294–95.

64. Foucault, "*Society Must Be Defended*," 243; see also 246, 249–50.

65. Esposito, *Bios*, 4.

66. Giorgio Agamben, *The Open: Man and Animal*, trans. Kevin Attell (Stanford, CA: Stanford University Press, 2004), 75.

67. Jacques Rancière, "Who Is the Subject of the Rights of Man?" *South Atlantic Quarterly* 103, nos. 2/3 (Spring/Summer 2004): 300.

68. Giorgio Agamben, *Homo Sacer: Sovereign Power and Bare Life*, trans. Daniel Heller-Roazen (Stanford, CA: Stanford University Press, 1998), 84.

69. Jonathan Elmer, "Torture and Hyperbole," *Law, Culture, and the Humanities* 3, no. 1 (2007): 20.

70. Ibid., 30.

71. Agamben, *Homo Sacer*, 133–34.

72. Rancière, "Who Is the Subject?" 301.

73. Agamben, *The Open*, 91.

74. Ibid., 92.

75. Dominick LaCapra, *History and Its Limits: Human, Animal, Violence* (Ithaca, NY: Cornell University Press, 2009), 167.

76. LaCapra, *History and Its Limits*, 165.

77. Laurent Dubreuil, "Leaving Politics: *Bios, Zoe*, Life," trans. Clarissa C. Eagle with the author, *Diacritics* 36, no. 2 (Summer 2006): 88. As he characterizes it, "Agamben's philology suggests disciplinary procedures, but it is *foremost* intended for the readers who do not possess the means of verification." Specifically, Agamben's valorization of the Greek "thus plays into an overall strategic approach. The number of readers capable of verifying case by case the arguments surrounding the Hellenic corpus is proportionally as slight as the risk contesting any of these" (ibid.). And this allows Agamben, in turn, to recast history as "more or less 'beginning,' or origin. One returns to the Greeks so as to plunge into the causality of the past," and "history is precisely a *fall* out of the initial paradise." Thus, "historical and local fractures are the hypostasis of an originary fissure in the origin" (ibid., 87).

78. Giorgio Agamben, *What Is an Apparatus? and Other Essays*, trans. David Kishik and Stefan Padatella (Stanford, CA: Stanford University Press, 2009), 11.

79. Ibid., 21.

80. Ibid., 23–24.

81. LaCapra, *History and Its Limits*, 166.

82. Ibid., 172.

83. Rancière, "Who Is the Subject?" 308.

84. Quoted in Elmer, "Torture and Hyperbole," 30–31.

85. Elmer, "Torture and Hyperbole," 31.

86. Rancière, "Who Is the Subject?" 309.

87. Badiou, quoted in Elmer, "Torture and Hyperbole," 31.

88. Elmer, "Torture and Hyperbole," 32.

89. Quoted in Elmer, "Torture and Hyperbole," 32.

90. Slavoj Zizek, "From Politics to Biopolitics . . . and Back," in *South Atlantic Quarterly* 102, nos. 2/3 (Spring/Summer 2004): 513.

91. Ibid., 512.

92. Ibid.

93. Ibid., 510–11.

94. Ibid., 512.

95. Ibid., 511.

96. John Baldwin, "Don't Worry, Be Happy: On 'Ethics as a Figure of Nihilism,'" *Subject Matters* 1, no. 2 (2004): 29.

97. Nick Haeffner, "The Ethic of Truths and Faith-Based Intelligence," *Subject Matters* 1, no. 2 (2004): 43. Haeffner's article also contains an engaging and illuminating discussion of Terry Eagleton's musings in his autobiography on why many people raised Catholic find the transition to Marxism an easy one to make. As LaCapra aptly describes it, in Žižek, Agamben, and Badiou, "a seemingly extreme leftism merges with an extreme conservatism reminiscent of theologians for whom the radical evil or ontologically warped nature of 'man' requires strict and even cruel normative strictures" (*History and Its Limits*, 43). As Simon Critchley and others have argued, the either/or-ism around the "genuinely political" in Badiou et al. is actually not "political" at all, since it is conceptually incapable of thinking the different political logic of the modern period to which Foucault's work—and not just Foucault's, of course—devotes itself (see Baldwin, "Don't Worry, Be Happy," 29–30), which is one reason for Foucault's own trajectory, as it moves from the model of "war" and "battle" early in "*Society Must Be Defended*" to thinking political effectivity in terms of the strategic and the compositional.

SECTION THREE

1. Niklas Luhmann, *Observations on Modernity*, trans. William Whobrey (Stanford, CA: Stanford University Press, 1998), 30.

2. Maurizio Lazzarato, "From Biopower to Biopolitics," *Pli* 13 (2002): 104.

3. Roberto Esposito, *Bios: Biopolitics and Philosophy*, trans. and intro. Timothy Campbell (Minneapolis: University of Minnesota Press, 2008), 28.

4. Jeffrey Nealon, *Foucault beyond Foucault: Power and Its Intensifications since 1984* (Stanford, CA: Stanford University Press, 2007), 46.

5. Roberto Esposito, *Immunitas: The Protection and Negation of Life* (London: Polity Press, 2011), 136.

6. Lazzarato, "From Biopower to Biopolitics," 101.

7. Ibid., 103.

8. Nealon, *Foucault beyond Foucault*, 37.

9. See, e.g., Esposito's discussion of Foucault's analysis of medicalization and urban space in Europe from around 1800 forward, in which the very processes that "make live" (to use Foucault's famous phrase) "contained something that internally contradicted it." As Esposito notes, "the first step is to isolate places where infectious germs may develop more easily due to the storage of bodies, whether dead or alive: ports, prisons, factories, hospitals, cemeteries." What is generated is a kind of "*quadrillage,* or pigieonholing, that placed individuals in an extensive system of institutional segments—family, school, army, factory, hospital—prohibiting, or at least controlling, circulation in the name of public safety. All the urbanization that developed in Europe starting in the middle of the eighteenth century took on the appearance of a dense network of fences between places, zones, and territories protected by boundaries established according to political and administrative rules that went well beyond sanitary needs" (*Immunitas*, 139–40).

10. In Foucault's words, "where there is power, there is resistance, and yet, or rather consequently, this resistance is never in a position of exteriority in relation to power" (quoted in Esposito, *Bios*, 38). See Gilles Deleuze, *Foucault*, trans. Sean Hand, foreword Paul Bové (Minneapolis: University of Minnesota Press, 1988), 71. See also Nealon, *Foucault beyond Foucault*, 38.

11. Lazzarato, "From Biopower to Biopolitics," 100. Rather than thinking of the "political" as essentially a logical problem, along the axis of the Schmitt/Agamben "decisionist" rendering of the "state of exception" in relation to sovereignty, we are better off, Andrew Norris suggests, in thinking of it along the lines of what Stanley Cavell, following Wittgenstein, calls "forms of life." As Norris puts it, for Cavell, "the criteria and the judgments that define our experience are not prior to that experience; the subject of responsibility is always *us*, here and now. . . . Criteria are applied by each one of us, and each one of us has to judge for him- or herself whether the others with them have judged by (acknowledged) the same criteria understood in the same way" (Andrew Norris, "The State of Exception as a Political and Logical Problem," lecture, Rice University, Houston, TX, Feb. 12, 2010). "Human speech and activity," Cavell writes, "sanity and community, rest on nothing more, but nothing less, than this. It is a vision as simple as it is difficult, and as difficult as it is (and because it is) terrifying" (Stanley Cavell, *Must We Mean What We Say?* [Cambridge: Cambridge University Press, 1969], 52). In contrast, as Norris notes, we will remember Agamben's assertion that

only the sovereign decision on the exception opens the space in which it is possible to trace borders between inside and outside and in which determinate rules can be assigned to determinate territories. In exactly the same way, only language as the pure potentiality to signify, withdrawing itself from every concrete instance of speech, divides the linguistic from the nonlinguistic and allows for the opening of areas of meaningful speech in which certain terms correspond to certain denotations. Language is the sovereign who, in a permanent state of exception, declares that there is nothing outside language and that language is always beyond itself. (Giorgio Agamben, *Homo Sacer: Sovereign Power and Bare Life*, trans. Daniel Heller-Roazen [Stanford, CA: Stanford University Press, 1998], 21)

But for Cavell, "the limits of our language are in no sense *metaphysical* limits," as Norris puts it, and so "the logical reading of the exception whereby something like a sovereign decision is called for by each of us each time we apply a rule" gives way to the realization of "the fragility of our agreement in language, and hence the fragility of our life," the fact "that our common life rests upon factors outside of our individual control," which drives us to believe "either that rules bind us together, or that acts of a sovereign or set of sovereigns will keep us together."

I think Norris is right, but what needs to be added here is that "forms of life" are better conceived as *dispositifs* that include but are not limited to a formalist and conventionalist rendering in terms of our language, our "agreements" and "criteria," and so on. Indeed, it is this sense of Foucault's term that Agamben teases out in the recent essay "What Is an Apparatus?" before eventually (as we have already noted) tethering it back to what he himself calls a "theological legacy" (Giorgio Agamben, *What Is an Apparatus? and Other Essays*, trans. David Kishik and Stefan Padatella [Stanford, CA: Stanford University Press, 2009], 11). There, Agamben notes that the *dispositif* is "a heterogeneous set that includes virtually anything, linguistic or nonlinguistic, under the same heading: discourses, institutions, buildings, laws, police measures, philosophical propositions, and so on. The apparatus itself is the network that is established between these elements" (ibid., 3). Indeed, he insists later in that same essay on "a general and massive partitioning of beings into two large groups or classes: on the one hand, living beings (or substances); and on the other, apparatuses in which living beings are incessantly captured" (ibid., 13). "And, between these two, as a third class," Agamben adds, "subjects. I call a subject that which results from the relation and, so to speak, from the relentless fight between living beings and apparatuses" (ibid., 14). Apparatuses "must always imply a process of subjectification, that is to say, they must produce their subject," and in this, he notes—in terms that now reach back to the very opening of this essay—the concept intersects "with what the later Heidegger callled *Gestell*" or "framing" (ibid., 11, 12).

12. Lazzarato, "From Biopower to Biopolitics," 104.

13. Ibid., 103.

14. Jacques Rancière, "Who Is the Subject of the Rights of Man?" *South Atlantic Quarterly* 103, nos. 2/3 (Spring/Summer 2004): 304.

15. Jacques Rancière, "Biopolitics or Politics?" in *Dissensus: On Politics and Aesthetics*, ed. and trans. Steven Corcoran (London: Continuum, 2010), 92–93.

16. Michel Foucault, "Power Affects the Body," in *Foucault Live: Collected Interviews 1961–1984*, ed. Sylvère Lotringer (New York: Semiotexte, 1989), 209.

17. Ibid.

18. Lazzarato, "From Biopower to Biopolitics," 107.

19. Ibid., 105–6.

20. Lewis Holloway and Carol Morris, "Contesting Genetic Knowledge-Practices in Livestock Breeding: Biopower, Biosocial Collectivities and Heterogeneous Resistances," *Environment and Planning 10: Society and Space* 30, no. 1 (forthcoming 2012).

21. Ibid.

22. Ibid.

23. Ibid.

24. Ibid.

25. Ibid.

26. Esposito, *Bios*, 39.

27. Ibid., 42.

28. Agamben, *Homo Sacer*, 166.

29. Esposito, *Bios*, 43.

30. Michel Foucault, *"Society Must Be Defended": Lectures at the Collège de France, 1975–1976*, ed. Mauro Bertani and Alessandro Fontana, trans. David Macey(New York: Picador, 2003), 255.

31. Esposito, *Bios*, 32; emphasis added.

32. Esposito, *Immunitas*, 136; see also 138.

33. Ibid., 127.

34. Esposito, *Bios*, 46.

35. Ibid., 56.

36. Ibid., 50.

37. Ibid., 46; see also Roberto Esposito, "The Person and Human Life," trans. Diana Garvin and Thomas Kelso, in *Theory after "Theory,"* ed. Jane Elliott and Derek Attridge (London: Routledge, 2011), 210–11.

38. Esposito, *Bios*, 60–61.

39. Esposito, "The Person and Human Life," 208, 210.

40. Ibid., 212.

41. Esposito, *Bios*, 47.

42. Ibid., 78, 81.

43. Ibid., 80.

44. Ibid., 83.

45. Ibid., 109.

46. Vanessa Lemm, *Nietzsche's Animal Philosophy: Culture, Politics, and the Animality of the Human Being* (New York: Fordham University Press, 2009), 3.

47. Ibid., 5.

48. Peter Sloterdijk, "Rules for the Human Zoo: A Response to the *Letter on Humanism*," trans. Mary Varney Rorty, *Society and Space* 27 (2009): 18.

49. Ibid., 22.

50. Esposito, "The Person and Human Life," 9.

51. Friedrich Balke, "From a Biopolitical Point of View: Nietzsche's Philosophy of Crime," *Cardozo Law Review* 24, no. 2 (2003): 709–10.

52. Ibid., 719–20.

53. Sloterdijk, "Rules for the Human Zoo," 23.

54. Jacques Derrida, *The Animal That Therefore I Am*, ed. Marie-Louise Mallet, trans. David Wills (New York: Fordham University Press, 2008), 47–48; Gilles Deleuze and Félix Guattari, *A Thousand Plateaus: Capitalism and Schizophrenia*, trans. Brian Massumi (Minneapolis: University of Minnesota Press, 1987), 239.

55. Quoted in Esposito, *Bios*, 98.

56. Esposito, *Bios*, 98.

SECTION FOUR

1. Michel Foucault, *"Society Must Be Defended": Lectures at the Collège de France, 1975–1976*, ed. Mauro Bertani and Alessandro Fontana, trans. David Macey (New York: Picador, 2003), 255–56.

2. Ibid., 256.

3. Ibid., 255.

4. Karen Davis, *The Holocaust and the Henmaid's Tale* (New York: Lantern Books, 2005), 11, 12.

5. Ibid., 5, 16.

6. Roberto Esposito, *Bios: Biopolitics and Philosophy*, trans. and intro. Timothy Campbell (Minneapolis: University of Minnesota Press, 2008), 129–30.

7. Peter Singer, "Ethics beyond Species and beyond Instincts: A Response to Richard Posner," in *Animal Rights: Current Debates and New Directions*, ed. Cass R. Sunstein and Martha C. Nussbaum (New York: Oxford University Press, 2004), 91 n. 12. Singer draws on Boria Sax, *Animals in the Third Reich: Pets, Scapegoats, and the Holocaust* (New York: Continuum, 2000).

8. Jacques Derrida, *The Animal That Therefore I Am*, ed. Marie-Louise Mallet, trans. David Wills (New York: Fordham University Press, 2008), 26.

9. As Agamben puts it, "Insofar as its inhabitants were stripped of every political status and wholly reduced to bare life, the camp was also the most absolute biopolitical space ever to have been realized, in which power confronts nothing but pure life, without any mediation" (Giorgio Agamben, *Homo Sacer: Sovereign Power and Bare Life*, trans. Daniel Heller-Roazen [Stanford, CA: Stanford University Press, 1998], 171).

10. Esposito, *Bios*, 137.

11. Derrida, *The Animal That Therefore I Am*, 26.

12. Humane Farming Association website, https://hfa.org/factory/index.html, last visited Sept. 8, 2008.

13. Davis, *Holocaust* , 9.

14. Charles Patterson, *Eternal Treblinka: Our Treatment of Animals and the Holocaust* (New York: Lantern Books, 2002), 53.

15. Ibid., 72.

16. Jacques Derrida, *The Beast and the Sovereign*, ed. Michel Lisse, Marie-Louise Mallet, and Ginette Michaud, trans. Geoffrey Bennington, vol. 1 (Chicago: University of Chicago Press, 2009), 71.

17. Ibid., 71–72. But as Derrida writes in "Faith and Knowledge" (glossing a critique he develops in more detail in *Politics of Friendship*), "Schmitt was obliged to acknowledge that the ostensibly purely political categories to which he resorted were the product of a secularization or of a theologico-political heritage. . . . Even supposing that one accepts such premises, the unprecedented forms of today's wars of religion could also imply radical challenges to our project of delimiting the political." Jacques Derrida, "Faith and Knowledge: Two Sources of 'Religion' at the Limits of Reason Alone," trans. Samuel Weber, in *Religion*, ed. Jacques Derrida and Gianni Vattimo (Stanford, CA: Stanford University Press, 1998), 26.

18. Penelope Deutscher, "The Inversion of Exceptionality: Foucault, Agamben, and 'Reproductive Rights,'" *South Atlantic Quarterly* 107, no. 1 (Winter 2008): 57.

19. Ibid., 59.

20. Ibid., 66–67.

21. Ibid., 59.

22. Ibid., 58.

23. Ibid., 67.

24. Nicholas D. Kristof, "Cleaning the Henhouse," *New York Times*, Sept. 1, 2010. Last accessed Sept. 3, 2010, www. nytimes.com/2010/09/02/opinion/02kristof.html.

25. Doug Gurian-Sherman, *CAFOs Uncovered: The Untold Costs of Confined Animal Feeding Operations*, Union of Concerned Scientists, April 2008, 65. Last accessed Nov. 25, 2010, http://www.ucsusa.org/assets/documents/food_and_agriculture/cafos-uncovered.pdf.

26. Nicholas D. Kristof, "When Food Kills," *New York Times*, June 12, 2011, Week In Review sec. 10.

27. Davis, *Holocaust*, 21–22.

28. Quoted in Roberto Esposito, *Immunitas: The Protection and Negation of Life* (London: Polity Press, 2011), 140–41.

29. Esposito, *Immunitas*, 141.

30. Ibid., 121.

31. On organization versus structure, see Humberto Maturana and Francisco

Varela, *The Tree of Knowledge: The Biological Roots of Human Understanding*, trans. Robert Paolucci, foreword by J. Z. Young, rev. ed. (Boston: Shambhala Press, 1992), 46–47.

32. Ibid.

33. Michel Foucault, "Power Affects the Body," in *Foucault Live: Collected Interviews 1961–1984*, ed. Sylvère Lotringer (New York: Semiotexte, 1989), 211.

34. Nicole Shukin, *Animal Capital: Rendering Life in Biopolitical Times* (Minneapolis: University of Minnesota Press, 2009), 11.

35. See Nikolas Rose, *The Politics of Life Itself: Biomedicine, Power, and Subjectivity in the Twenty-First Century* (Princeton, NJ: Princeton University Press, 2007), in particular 255, 167, 257; and the rewriting of biopolitics in terms of human labor-power in Paolo Virno, *A Grammar of the Multitude*, trans. Isabella Bertoletti et al., foreword Sylvère Lotringer (New York: Semiotexte, 2004), 81–84.

36. Shukin, *Animal Capital*, 7.

37. Ibid., 12.

38. Ibid., 46.

39. Matthew Calarco, *Zoographies: The Question of the Animal from Heidegger to Derrida* (New York: Columbia University Press, 2008), 97.

SECTION FIVE

1. See Paul Greenberg, "Tuna's End," *New York Times Magazine*, June 22, 2010, MM28.

2. Statistics provided by American Pet Products Manufacturer's Association, last accessed Sept. 10, 2008, www.fetchpetcare.com, and Lana Berkowitz, "Pets Are a Booming Industry," *Houston Chronicle*, Feb. 23, 2010; last accessed August 5, 2010, http://www.chron.com/disp/story.mpl/pets/6881710.html.

3. On the Missyplicity Project, see Donna J. Haraway, *When Species Meet* (Minneapolis: University of Minnesota Press, 2008), 151–53.

4. Berkowitz, "Pets Are a Booming Industry."

5. Ibid.

6. James Vlahos, "Pill-Popping Pets," *New York Times Magazine*, July 13, 2008, 40.

7. Ibid., 54.

8. Ibid., 40.

9. Ibid., 62.

10. Rosi Braidotti, *Transpositions* (Cambridge: Polity, 2006), 100.

11. Ibid.

12. Roberto Esposito, *Bios: Biopolitics and Philosophy*, trans. and intro. Timothy Campbell (Minneapolis: University of Minnesota Press, 2008), 180.

13. Ibid., 192.

14. Ibid., 188.

15. As Bateson puts it in a key passage from the seminal essay "Form, Substance, and Difference" that has considerable resonance with Esposito's deployment of both Nietzsche and Simondon,

> The unit of survival is not the breeding organism, or the family line, or the society. The old unit has already been partly corrected by the population geneticists. They have insisted that the evolutionary unit is, in fact, not homogeneous. A wild population of any species consists always of individuals whose genetic constitution varies widely. In other words, potentiality and readiness for change is already built into the survival unit. The heterogeneity of the wild population is already one-half of that trial-and-error system which is necessary for dealing with environment. . . .
>
> And today a further correction of the unit is necessary. The flexible environment must also be included along with the flexible organism because, as I have already said, the organism which destroys its environment destroys itself. The unit of survival is a flexible organism-in-its-environment. (Gregory Bateson, *Steps to an Ecology of Mind* [New York: Ballantine, 1972], 451)

16. This is not by any means only Esposito's problem. Even in Derrida's work, we find a tension or slippage between his careful differentiation of forms of life and the "multiplicity of heterogeneous structures and limits" that obtain among living beings, on the one hand, and a countervailing tendency to speak of "the living in general" on the other (Jacques Derrida, *The Animal That Therefore I Am*, ed. Marie-Louise Mallet, trans. David Wills [New York: Fordham University Press, 2008], 48).

17. Eugene Thacker, *After Life* (Chicago: University of Chicago Press, 2010), 234.

18. Ibid.

19. Martin Hägglund, "The Arche-Materiality of Time: Deconstruction, Evolution and Speculative Materialism," in *Theory after "Theory,"* ed. Jane Elliott and Derek Attridge (London: Routledge, 2011), 265.

20. Jacques Derrida, *Without Alibi*, ed. and trans. Peggy Kamuf (Stanford, CA: Stanford University Press, 2002), 136.

21. Hägglund, "The Arche-Materiality of Time," 272–73. "Far from metaphysical" for the following reason: "the deconstructive notion of the trace is logical rather than ontological. Accordingly, my argument does not assume the form of an unconditional assertion ('being is spacing, hence arche-materiality') but rather the form of a conditional claim ('if your discourse commits you to a notion of succession, then you are committed to a notion of spacing and hence arche-materiality'). The discourse in question can then be ontological, epistemological, phenomenological, or scientific—in all these cases the logic of the trace will have expressive power insofar as there is an implicit or explicit commitment to a notion of succession" (ibid., 270).

22. Quoted in. Ibid., 275.

23. Ibid.

24. Roberto Esposito, *Immunitas: The Protection and Negation of Life* (London: Polity Press, 2011), 136.

25. Roberto Esposito, "The Person and Human Life," trans. Diana Garvin and Thomas Kelso, in *Theory after "Theory,"* ed. Jane Elliott and Derek Attridge (London: Routledge, 2011), 218; emphasis added.

26. Esposito, *Immunitas*, 112.

27. Esposito, "The Person and Human Life," 217–18.

28. Thacker, *After Life*, 240.

29. Esposito, "The Person and Human Life," 218.

30. Tim Luke, "The Dreams of Deep Ecology," *Telos* 76 (Summer 1988): 51.

31. Esposito, *Bios*, 186.

32. Ibid., 187.

33. Richard Rorty, "Postmodern Bourgeois Liberalism," in *Objectivity, Relativism, and Truth: Philosophical Papers*, vol. 1 (Cambridge: Cambridge University Press, 1991), 198. For a discussion of these questions in relation to biocentrism and deep ecology, see Murray Bookchin and Dave Foreman, *Defending the Earth: A Dialogue between Murray Bookchin and Dave Foreman*, ed. and intro. Steve Chase, foreword David Levine (Boston: South End Press, 1991), 123–27.

34. Luke, "Dreams of Deep Ecology," 51.

35. Patrick Curry, *Ecological Ethics: An Introduction* (Cambridge: Polity, 2006), 75–76.

36. "Biology 2.0," *Economist*, June 19, 2010, 4.

37. Ibid.

38. "Genesis Redux," *Economist*, May 22, 2010, 81–82.

39. Ibid., 82.

40. See Michael Specter, "Annals of Science: A Life of Its Own," *New Yorker*, Sept. 28, 2009, 65.

41. Jacques Derrida, *Rogues: Two Essays on Reason*, trans. Pascale-Anne Brault and Michael Naas (Stanford, CA: Stanford University Press, 2005), 146–47.

42. Ibid., 147.

SECTION SIX

1. Claire Colebrook, "Creative Evolution and the Creation of Man," in *After-Life: Extinction in Theory*, unpublished manuscript, 15.

2. Jacques Derrida, *Without Alibi*, ed. and trans. Peggy Kamuf (Stanford, CA: Stanford University Press, 2002), 136.

3. See Cary Wolfe, *What Is Posthumanism?* (Minneapolis: University of Minnesota Press, 2010), chap. 2.

4. Jacques Derrida, *The Animal That Therefore I Am*, ed. Marie-Louise Mallet, trans. David Wills (New York: Fordham University Press, 2008), 135.

5. Ibid., 135–36.

6. Ibid., 124.

7. Ibid., 138.

8. Jacques Derrida, *The Beast and the Sovereign*, ed. Michel Lisse, Marie-Louise Mallet, and Ginette Michaud, trans. Geoffrey Bennington, vol. 1 (Chicago: University of Chicago Press, 2009), 154.

9. Ibid. What we find here, in fact, is Deleuze's version of Bataille's position in *Theory of Religion*, that "the animal" moves through the world "like water in water" and lives in a world of immanence. George Bataille, *Theory of Religion*, trans. Robert Hurley (New York: Zone Books, 1989), 19.

10. Derrida, *The Beast and the Sovereign*, 178.

11. Ibid., 181; emphasis added.

12. Ibid.

13. Ibid., 183.

14. See Lydia Liu, "The Cybernetic Unconscious: Rethinking Lacan, Poe, and French Theory," *Critical Inquiry* 36, no. 2 (Winter 2010): 288–320.

15. Derrida, *The Beast and the Sovereign*, 183.

16. Derrida, *The Animal That Therefore I Am*, 30.

17. Derrida, *The Beast and the Sovereign*, 183; emphasis added.

18. But see in this regard Stuart Elden's essay "Heidegger's Animals," which notes that in Heidegger's body of work "the range of animals discussed is extensive" and they are "not merely tangential references, but part of an extensive analysis that draws on a number of works in contemporary biology," including those by Hans Driesh and Jakob von Uexküll (*Continental Philosophy Review* 39 [2006]: 274–75).

19. Vinciane Despret, "The Body We Care For: Figures of Anthropo-zoo-genesis," *Body and Society* 10, nos. 2–3 (2004): 118.

20. Ibid.

21. Ibid., 119.

22. Ibid., 122. By way of contrast, Despret reminds us of the infamous "well of despair" experiments that Harry Harlow carried out on rhesus monkeys in the early 1960s, in which the young monkeys were deprived of any bodily contact, maternal or otherwise. Here, rather than being interacted with and encouraged in ways that make possible the emergence of a new kind of identity by means of "an apparatus that is designed to give the opportunity to the 'subject' of the experiment to show what are the most interesting questions to address to him; what are the questions that make him/her the most articulate," the animals are "articulated by the apparatus in such a way that there is no one to raise the question of the 'point of view,' the question of what 'makes sense' for a rhesus monkey." For Despret, the takeaway lesson here is "the contrast between a scientist who relies on the availability of both the apparatus

and the animal, and a scientist who requires docility (this scientist being himself docile to the perceived prerequisites of science)" (ibid., 124).

23. Gordon M. Burghardt, *The Genesis of Animal Play: Testing the Limits* (Cambridge, MA: MIT Press, 2005), 397. Burghardt's claim may seem a bold one, but in fact it is shared by leading researchers in primatology and communication such as Barbara J. King and Michael Tomasello (though it should be noted that the Derridean perspective would be closer to King's theoretical framework of developmental systems theory and her emphasis on distributed cognition and social coordination and coregulation rather than Tomasello's emphasis on iconicity and intentionality). See Barbara J. King, *The Dynamic Dance: Nonvocal Communication in African Great Apes* (Cambridge, MA: Harvard University Press. 2004), 60, 99–101.

24. José Luis Bermúdez, *Thinking without Words* (Oxford: Oxford University Press, 2003), 3.

25. Ibid., 4.

26. King, *Dynamic Dance*, 66.

27. Quoted in. Ibid., 77.

28. Alva Noë, *Out of Our Heads: Why You Are Not Your Brain, and Other Lessons from the Biology of Consciousness* (New York: Hill and Wang, 2009), xiii.

29. Ibid., 43.

30. Humberto Maturana and Francisco Varela, *The Tree of Knowledge: The Biological Roots of Human Understanding*, trans. Robert Paolucci, foreword by J. Z. Young, rev. ed. (Boston: Shambhala Press, 1992), 180.

31. Ibid., 193.

32. For a useful and rather different exploration of neurophysiological plasticity, see Catherine Malabou, *What Shall We Do with Our Brain?* trans. Sebastian Rand, foreword Marc Jeannerod (New York: Fordham University Press, 2008). As she notes, three distinct kinds of plasticity are relevant here: "1) the modeling of neuronal connections (developmental plasticity in the embryo and the child); 2) the modification of neuronal connections (the plasticity of synaptic modulation throughout life); and 3) the capacity for repair (post-lesional plasticity)" (5).

33. I have discussed these questions in more detail in Cary Wolfe, *Animal Rites: American Culture, the Discourse of Species, and Posthumanist Theory* (Chicago: University of Chicago Press, 2003), 78–94, a discussion from which I borrow here.

34. King, *Dynamic Dance*, 222.

35. Gregory Bateson, *Steps to an Ecology of Mind* (New York: Ballantine, 1972), 181.

36. Ibid., 182.

37. Ibid.

38. Daniel Dennett, *Consciousness Explained* (Boston: Little, Brown, 1991), 450. I have discussed Dennett's work and some of its problems both in *Animal Rites*, 88–89, and, in more detail, in *What Is Posthumanism?* chap 2.

39. Burghardt, *Genesis of Animal Play* , 372–74.

40. Eric Scigliano, "Through the Eye of an Octopus," *Discover* (October 2003), last accessed July 22, 2011, http://discovermagazine.com/2003/oct/feateye.

41. Ibid.

SECTION SEVEN

1. Jacques Derrida, *The Animal That Therefore I Am*, ed. Marie-Louise Mallet, trans. David Wills (New York: Fordham University Press, 2008), 30.

2. Ibid.

3. Dominick LaCapra, *History and Its Limits: Human, Animal, Violence* (Ithaca, NY: Cornell University Press, 2009), 127.

4. Jacques Derrida, *Of Spirit: Heidegger and the Question*, trans. Geoffrey Bennington and Rachel Bowlby (Chicago: University of Chicago Press, 1989), 57.

5. Derrida, *The Animal That Therefore I Am*, 29.

6. Ibid., 30–31.

7. Matthew Calarco, *Zoographies: The Question of the Animal from Heidegger to Derrida* (New York: Columbia University Press, 2008), 89–90.

8. Jacques Derrida and Elisabeth Roudinesco, *For What Tomorrow: A Dialogue*, trans. Jeff Fort (Stanford, CA: Stanford University Press, 2004), 63.

9. Martin Hägglund, "The Arche-Materiality of Time: Deconstruction, Evolution and Speculative Realism," in *Theory after "Theory,"* ed. Jane Elliott and Derek Attridge (London: Routledge, 2011), 265.

10. Richard Beardsworth, *Derrida and the Political* (London: Routledge, 1996), 103.

11. Hägglund, "Arche-Materiality of Time," 272.

12. Beardsworth, *Derrida and the Political*, 151.

13. David Wills, "Techneology or the Discourse of Speed," in *The Prosthetic Impulse: From a Posthuman Present to a Biocultural Future*, ed. Marquard Smith and Joanne Morra (Cambridge, MA: MIT Press, 2006), 241.

14. Bernard Stiegler, *Technics and Time*, vol. 1: *The Fault of Epimetheus*, trans. Richard Beardsworth and George Collins (Stanford, CA: Stanford University Press, 1998), 179.

15. But for a brief indication of just how vexed this question is, the reader may consult the section "The Language of the Almost Human" in. Ibid., 164–69; see also 144–46.

16. For brief evidence of which see, e.g., Mike Hansell, *Built by Animals: The Natural History of Animal Architecture* (Oxford: Oxford University Press, 2009), esp. 180–215.

17. Humberto Maturana and Francisco Varela, *The Tree of Knowledge: The Biological Roots of Human Understanding*, trans. Robert Paolucci, foreword by J. Z. Young, rev. ed. (Boston: Shambhala Press, 1992), 45.

18. Stiegler, *Technics and Time*, 149. Here, however, it is worth remembering David Wills's observation that in Stiegler's work, language "is not subjected to the same examination" as other items in the nexus of technics—corticalization, verticality, mobility, and time—"and so remains, in the final analysis, instrumental to technology, simply words processed by that technology," whereas what is wanted is "some sort of analysis of the technological logic of its operations beyond a simple mechanics of its syntax and semantics." David Wills, *Dorsality: Thinking Back through Technology and Politics* (Minneapolis: University of Minnesota Press, 2008), 15.

19. Jacques Derrida, *Of Grammatology*, trans. Gayatri Chakravorty Spivak (Baltimore: Johns Hopkins University Press, 1976), 84.

20. Ibid.

21. See Gordon M. Burghardt, *The Genesis of Animal Play: Testing the Limits* (Cambridge, MA: MIT Press, 2005), 382, 397. And it is also worth remembering, as Hansell points out, that there is a far from direct correlation between tool use and intelligence in nonhuman animals (a fact made even more complicated by the theoretical and methodological questions of how we construe the relationship between tool use and the creation of built structures in animals since, after all, many of the most elaborate and impressive built structures in the animal world are made by creatures, such as social insects, with minimal cephalization and behavioral plasticity). In fact, taking only the example of the great apes, Hansell notes that chimpanzees are impressive tool users in the wild, but bonobos, orangutans, and gorillas are not. And yet orangutans in captivity, once freed of the demands of life in the trees, rival chimpanzees in their complex interactions with a range of tools (Hansell, *Built by Animals*, 189, 209).

22. Barbara J. King, "What Apes, Elephants, and Corvids Tell Us (and Can't Tell Us) about Humanism," lecture, Williams College, Williamstown, MA, Sept. 23, 2010.

23. Beardsworth, *Derrida and the Political*, 152.

24. Giorgio Agamben, *The Open: Man and Animal*, trans. Kevin Attell (Stanford, CA: Stanford University Press, 2004), 91.

25. Ibid., 70.

26. See my discussion of Žižek's schema and its problems in Cary Wolfe, *What Is Posthumanism?* (Minneapolis: University of Minnesota Press, 2010), 180–202.

27. As we have already seen in Derrida's discussion of the unconscious in *The Beast and the Sovereign*, this provides a point of connection with psychoanalysis, though it need not be, as with Žižek, either limited to it or to a dialectical schema.

28. LaCapra, *History and Its Limits*, 127.

29. Ibid., 127–28.

30. Stuart Elden, "Heidegger's Animals," *Continental Philosophy Review* 39 (2006): 274.

31. David Farrell Krell, *Daimon Life: Heidegger and Life-Philosophy* (Bloomington: Indiana University Press, 1992), 275.

32. Ibid.

33. Ibid.

34. Derrida, *The Animal That Therefore I Am*, 151.

35. Ibid., 155.

36. See Wolfe, *What Is Posthumanism?* 78–98.

37. Derrida, *The Animal That Therefore I Am*, 39.

38. Derrida and Roudinesco, *For What Tomorrow*, 63.

39. Derrida, *Of Spirit*, 130 n. 5.

40. Ibid., 129–30 n. 5. As David Ferrell Krell notes, "questioning is the piety of thinking" in "The Question Concerning Technology" and "the exemplary interrogating-interrogated being" in *Being and Time*, and it is not "until very late in the day," in "The Essence of Language," that "Heidegger challenged the supreme dignity of the question by asserting the preeminence of the address and assent of and to language (*Zuspruch, Zusage*), language prior to all explicit questioning" (*Daimon Life*, 266). And Krell too notes the importance of the long endnote in *Of Spirit* discussed above in this regard, which he takes up with a rather different emphasis from mine later in his discussion of Derrida's text.

41. Derrida, *Of Spirit*, 134 n. 5.

42. Ibid.

43. Derrida, *The Animal That Therefore I Am*, 166 n. 36. Similarly, Derrida observes in the chapter devoted to Heidegger later in *The Animal That Therefore I Am* that the possibility of a "non-apophantic moment in the *logos*" identified by Aristotle and referenced by Heidegger would "open a breach in the whole apparatus," and for the very same reason. If the apophantic mode of questioning concerns the access to the "as such" of being that is barred, Heidegger argues, to animals—the sun doesn't appear to the lizard "*as* sun"—the possibility of a "non-apophantic marking (and I wouldn't say *logos* here), for example prayer, which doesn't show anything, which in a certain way 'doesn't say anything,'" refers to "a moment that isn't declarative, enunciative," as Aristotle puts it—a moment, that is, without the "question," without "response," and one that is (as Derrida's example of "prayer, which doesn't show anything" suggests), radically of the order of the *performative*, and hence has the same consequences for intentionality and response that Derrida outlines in "Signature Event Context" (ibid., 156–57). Jacques Derrida, "Signature Event Context," trans. Samuel Weber and Jeffrey Mehlman, in *Limited Inc*, ed. Gerald Graff (Evanston, IL: Northwestern University Press), 13–15. On these grounds, I would defend Derrida's angle of approach in *Of Spirit* against Krell's suggestion that Derrida "emphasizes Heidegger's hostility to *Lebensphilosophie*, emphasizes it perhaps excessively, inasmuch as Heidegger's discomfiture with transcendental phenomenology and his advance through *Existensphilosophie* to fundamental ontology

has much to do with his early conviction that philosophy must flourish on the basis of factical life and be at one with it" (273).

44. Jacques Derrida, "Eating Well," or the Calculation of the Subject: An Interview with Jacques Derrida," in *Who Comes After the Subject?* ed. Eduardo Cadava, Peter Connor, and Jean-Luc Nancy, trans. Peter Connor and Avital Ronnell (New York: Routledge, 1991), 100.

45. Ibid.

46. Martin Hägglund , *Radical Atheism: Derrida and the Time of Life* (Stanford, CA: Stanford University Press, 2008), 96.

47. Ibid., 94.

48. Ibid., 97.

49. Jane Bennett is quite right that "the philosophical project of naming where subjectivity begins and ends is too often bound up with fantasies of a human uniqueness in the eyes of God, of escape from materiality, or of mastery of nature; and even where it is not, it remains an aporetic or quixotic endeavor." It is that aporia that I am trying to address in the foregoing, and in a manner that I think is consonant with Bennett's observation that she is courting "the charge of performative self-contradiction: is it not a human subject who, after all, is articulating this theory of vibrant matter? Yes and no, for I will argue that what looks like a performative contradiction may well dissipate if one considers revisions in operative notions of matter, life, self, self-interest, will, and agency" — her version, in short, of what I have been articulating here as the prosthetic relation of the "who" and the "what." Jane Bennett,*Vibrant Matter: A Political Ecology of Things* (Durham, NC: Duke University Press, 2010), ix. Bruno Latour's formulation appears in *We Have Never Been Modern*, trans. Catherine Porter (Cambridge, MA: Harvard University Press, 1993).

50. "Infinite" here should be taken, of course, not in the sense of "positive infinity" that Derrida criticizes in Emmanuel Levinas's work but rather in the sense of the "infinite finitude of *différance*" that constitutes the alterity of a "who" who is also always already "other" to itself, constituted by what it is not (the trace, technicity, and so on) (Hägglund, *Radical Atheism*, 95, 94).

51. Dale Jamieson, "Animal Liberation Is an Environmental Ethic," *Environmental Values* 7 (1998): 41–57.

52. Ibid.

53. Ibid., 43–44.

54. Levi Bryant, "Questions about the Possibility of Non-Correlationist Ethics," *Larval Subjects* blog, last accessed July 23, 2011, http://larvalsubjects.wordpress .com/2010/01/28/questions-about-the-possibility-of-non-correlationist-ethics/.

55. With regard to the varieties of "response" and "transversal" relations in service animals, see Rebecca Skloot, "Creature Comforts," *New York Times Magazine*, Jan. 4, 2009; last accessed July 15, 2011, online: http://www.nytimes.com/2009/01/ 04/magazine/04Creatures-t.html?scp=1&sq=creature%20comforts&st=cse. There

are suggestive points of overlap here with Bryant's speculation that "when we relate to something we literally become a different entity," that "An entity that enters into a relational network with a hammer or a computer has *different* powers and capacities than an entity that does not exist in these relations and is, therefore, by this logic, a different entity. In ethical terms they are literally different *agents.*" A consequence of this is "that the ethico-politico domain is no longer a domain pertaining to the human, nor was it ever a domain pertaining to the human," and another "is that the ethico-politico domain *has never* been a homogeneous domain, but has always been a domain pertaining to diverse or heterogeneous entities pertaining to issues of how these entities are to relate to one another." He concludes, "If ontologically we cannot presuppose the formal identity of agents across diversity—indeed, if we cannot even presuppose *our own* identity by virtue of the fact that we become new agencies when we enter into new relations—*rule-based* ethical systems are out the window. . . . Yet if the domain of the ethical is not the domain of rules that would allow us to evaluate particular circumstances according to universal rules, then what is it? Perhaps, rather than judgment, the domain of the ethico-politico field is the domain not of *judgment,* but of *problematizations.*" I would largely agree but would fine-tune Bryant's position in the following way: we don't need the either/or-ism of "literally different agents" here; we can simply say that we are and are not the same agents depending on the context. Bryant's "pre-hammer" entity does not vanish when the hammer is picked up (and if he did, he, naturalistically speaking, couldn't pick up the hammer in the first place). We are (to put it in Derrida-ese) constituted by différance pre- and post-hammer. Second, I would agree that rule-based ethical systems are indeed "out the window," and that the ethico-political field becomes the domain of what Derrida calls "undecidability" and "pragmatic instances" (about which more in the next section). Bryant, "Questions about the Possibility of Non-Correlationist Ethics," last accessed July 23, 2011, at http://larvalsubjects.wordpress.com/2010/01/28/questions-about-the-possibility-of-non-correlationist-ethics.

56. And I would add—as I've suggested elsewhere—that there is no reason in principle that the "to whom" need be limited to organic or carbon-based life forms alone: a prospect which science fiction has of course explored for some time. I hasten to add here that this does *not* mean that the issue of embodiment is not important, or that the proverbial fantasies of "downloading your brain" by Hans Moravec and others (rightly criticized by Katherine Hayles) make any sense. The relevant question, which I cannot explore in detail here, would be the mode of embodiment in relation to recursive developmental change that allows not just requisite plasticity in the organism's individual ontogeny, but also, and therefore, its ability to thereby enter into an essentially prosthetic relation to the external technicities of code, semiosis, archive, and so on—regardless of whether the organism is made of "flesh and blood" or silicon and silicone. See the introduction to Wolfe, *What Is Posthumanism?*

57. Roberto Esposito, *Bios: Biopolitics and Philosophy,* trans. and intro. Timothy Campbell (Minneapolis: University of Minnesota Press, 2008), 187.

58. Ibid., 186.

59.Quoted in. Ibid., 186.

60. Ibid., 94.

SECTION EIGHT

1. See Cary Wolfe, *What Is Posthumanism?* (Minneapolis: University of Minnesota Press, 2010), chap. 1.

2. Jacques Derrida, *Rogues: Two Essays on Reason*, trans. Pascale-Anne Brault and Michael Naas (Stanford, CA: Stanford University Press, 2005), 85.

3. Niklas Luhmann, *Social Systems*, trans. John Bednarz Jr. with Dirk Baecker, foreword Eva M. Knodt (Stanford, CA: Stanford University Press, 1995), 375–76.

4. Ibid., 258.

5. Bruno Latour, "To Modernize or Ecologize? That Is the Question," in *Technoscience: The Politics of Interventions*, ed. Kristen Asdal et al. (Oslo: Oslo Academic Press, 2007), 264. For a full discussion of these and related ideas in Latour, see his *Reassembling the Social: An Introduction to Actor-Network Theory* (Oxford: Oxford University Press, 2007).

6. Gunther Teubner, "Rights of Non-humans? Electronic Agents and Animals as New Actors in Politics and Law," *Journal of Law and Society* 33, no. 4 (Dec. 2006): 518.

7. Ibid., 518.

8. Ibid., 519.

9. Ibid., 520.

10. Ibid.

11. Ibid.

12. Ibid.

13. Ibid., 515.

14.Roberto Esposito, *Bios: Biopolitics and Philosophy*, trans. and intro. Timothy Campbell (Minneapolis: University of Minnesota Press, 2008), 49.

15. Luhmann, *Social Systems*, 375.

16. Gunther Teubner, "Dealing with Paradoxes of Law: Derrida, Luhmann, Wietholter," trans. Iain L. Fraser, in *Paradoxes and Inconsistencies in the Law*, ed. Oren Perez and Gunther Teubner (Oxford: Hart, 2005): 60.

17. William Rasch, *Niklas Luhmann's Modernity: The Paradoxes of Differentiation* (Stanford, CA: Stanford University Press, 2000), 146.

18. Ibid., 148. As Rasch notes, "If we remain within the immanence of systems that Luhmann not only advocates but sees as inescapable, we are left with this paradox. Ethics emerges as the by-product of a system's attempt to preserve its own reproduction from the ravages of moral infection. The only moral preselection said to be ethically permissible is the preselection that guarantees the freedom of selec-

tion" (149). Here we find Luhmann's final take on a paradox of ethics familiar to us from Jean-François Lyotard's work: namely, that in the ethical task of respecting and preserving the "differends" that obtain between discrete and singular "language games," the only language game that is privileged is the one (namely ethics) that says "thou shalt not privilege one language game over another" (ibid., 92). It is precisely this rescue of the authority of ethics and an ethical imperative in some more-than-immanent (if not, in Lyotard, quite transcendental) sense that Luhmann's work is calculated to short-circuit. Because for Luhmann communications, and not concrete individuals, subjects, or social actors, are the basic elements of social systems, Rasch notes that "the notion of systemic closure and functional differentiation can be conveyed by saying that the 'language' of one system cannot be adequately translated into the 'language' of another system. Much like Wittgenstein's language games or Lyotard's genres, Luhmann's system languages are incommensurable, a fact that guarantees their autonomy (or, as Lyotard would say, a fact that guarantees the lack of a grand, totalizing narrative)" (ibid., 145).

19. Jacques Derrida, "Force of Law: The 'Mystical Foundation of Authority,'" trans. Mary Quaintance, *Cardozo Law Review* 11 (1990): 943.

20. Ibid., 941. In his analysis of Freud's *Totem and Taboo* in "Before the Law"—and here the points of connection with Luhmann's account of law become even clearer—Derrida demonstrates, as Richard Beardsworth puts it, that "the origin of law is an 'impossible' invention, and the condition of all inventions of law." Freud's attempt to account for the origin of law in the guilt and sin surrounding the primal patricide of *Totem and Taboo* "narrates an event that never takes place as such. For the brothers to feel guilty for the murder of their father, the moral law would *already* have to be in place prior to the crime. To have felt remorse the brothers must have already transgressed a prior law, not produced it; otherwise their remorse is incomprehensible." Richard Beardsworth, *Derrida and the Political* (London: Routledge, 1996), 31.

21. Derrida, "Force of Law," 949; see also 961–63.

22. As an example of the sort of pragmatic instance of the law iteration that Derrida identifies, we might point to the discourse of "human rights" which is often invoked in contemporary discussions as a counter to increasingly unequal effects of globalization—that is to say, invoked as an instance of immunitary closure and protection. That iteration of the principle of justice, however—as we have already seen in our discussion of Arendt—immediately begs the question that Derrida will not let us ignore: why *human* rights? What is it that is taken to be "proper" to the human, securing its ontological and ethical standing, that is barred to all other forms of life? As Derrida writes in *Rogues*, "It is rational, for example, at the very moment of endorsing, developing, perfecting, and determining human rights to continue to interrogate in a deconstructive fashion all the limits we thought pertained to life, the being of life and the life of being (and this is almost the entire history of philosophy), between the living and the dead, the living present and its spectral others, but also

between that living being called 'human' and the one called 'animal.'" Jacques Derrida, *Rogues*, 151.

23. Beardsworth, *Derrida and the Political*, 28.

24. Martin Hägglund, *Radical Atheism: Derrida and the Time of Life* (Stanford, CA: Stanford University Press, 2008), 41–42.

25. On "openness from closure," see the introduction to Wolfe, *What Is Posthumanism?*

26. *Philosophy in a Time of Terror: Dialogues with Jürgen Habermas and Jacques Derrida*, ed. Giovanna Borradori (Chicago: University of Chicago Press, 2003), 128–29.

27. Ibid., 129.

28. Ibid.

29. Ibid., 129–30.

30. See Cary Wolfe, *Critical Environments: Postmodern Theory and the Pragmatics of the "Outside"* (Minneapolis: University of Minnesota Press, 1998), chap. 3.

31. Derrida, "Force of Law," 932–33.

32. Paul Patton, "Future Politics," in *Between Deleuze and Derrida*, ed. Paul Patton and John Protevi (London: Continuum, 2003), 15, 16, 17.

33. See Borradori, *Philosophy in a Time of Terror*, 34, and Hägglund, *Radical Atheism*, 43.

34. Patton, "Future Politics," 24, 22.

35. Ibid., 22.

36. Ibid.

37. Derrida, *Rogues*, 84.

38. Ibid., 152. And here, we need to remember a point I emphasized in the previous section: that the term "vulnerability" in Derrida's late work references not just the finitude we experience as embodied beings; it also names the *double* finitude, the performativity and autoimmunity, whereby we are subjected to the *machinalité* of semiotic code, archive, and iterable trace. In that light, we can better appreciate his declaration later in that same text that "It is a question here, as with the coming of any event worthy of this name, of an unforeseeable coming of the other, of a heteronomy, of a law come from the other, of a responsibility and decision of the other—*of the other in me, an other greater and older than I am*" (ibid., 84; emphasis added).

39. See also in this connection Jacques Derrida, *The Beast and the Sovereign*, ed. Michel Lisse, Marie-Louise Mallet, and Ginette Michaud, trans. Geoffrey Bennington, vol. 1 (Chicago: University of Chicago Press, 2009), 73–74.

40. Jacques Derrida, "Faith and Knowledge: Two Sources of 'Religion' at the Limits of Reason Alone," in *Religion*, ed. Jacques Derrida and Gianni Vattimo, trans. Samuel Weber (Stanford, CA: Stanford University Press, 1998), 28.

41. Ibid., 48. In fact, as he notes, "the *phallos*, which is not the penis," "first designated in Greece and Rome for certain ceremonies, that simulacrum, that figure presentation of an erect penis, hard, stiff, rigid, precisely like a gigantic and arti-

ficially made-up puppet, made of tensed springs and exhibited during rituals and processions" (Derrida, *The Beast and the Sovereign*, 222).

42. Derrida, *The Beast and the Sovereign*, 222.

43. Ibid., 223.

44. Hägglund, *Radical Atheism*, 181.

45. Derrida, "Faith and Knowledge," 42.

46. Derrida, *Rogues*, 45; Jacques Derrida, *The Animal That Therefore I Am*, ed. Marie-Louise Mallet, trans. David Wills (New York: Fordham University Press, 2008), 47, 49–50; Jacques Derrida, "Eating Well," or the Calculation of the Subject: An Interview with Jacques Derrida," trans. Peter Connor and Avital Ronnell, in *Who Comes after the Subject?* ed. Eduardo Cadava, Peter Connor, and Jean-Luc Nancy (New York: Routledge, 1991), 114.

47. Derrida, "Eating Well," 112–13.

48. Ibid., 114.

49. Ibid., 113. Derrida's analysis of sovereignty and carnophallogocentrism is borne out by what I'm guessing is a very common experience among vegetarians: that when you tell people you don't eat meat, you are more likely to find acceptance if you say "It's against my religion" than if you try and offer a reasoned analytical explanation along the lines of a Peter Singer or a Tom Regan (animals are such and such kinds of beings, with such and such characteristics that we take to be relevant to moral standing, and so on). For more traditional analyses of the phallic character and heavily gendered topology of meat, see Carol J. Adams, *The Sexual Politics of Meat*, rev. ed. (London: Continuum, 2010) and Nick Fiddes, *Meat: A Natural Symbol* (London: Routledge, 1992).

50. D. J. Siegel, "In Search of a Test-Tube Hamburger," April 23, 2008, last accessed July 23, 2011, http://www.time.com/time/health/article/0,8599,1734630,00 .html.

51. I. Datar and M. Betti, "Possibilities for an In Vitro Meat Production System," *Innovative Food Science and Emerging Technologies* 11, no. 1 (Jan. 2010): 14, 22; Michael Specter, "Test-Tube Burgers," *New Yorker* (May 23, 2011), 34.

52. See Peter Singer, *Animal Liberation* (New York: Harper Perennial, 2009), and Martha C. Nussbaum, *Frontiers of Justice: Disability, Nationality, Species Membership* (Cambridge, MA: Harvard University Press, 2007). In this connection, it is useful to remember Tom Regan's thought experiment in *The Case for Animal Rights* which he brings to bear against the argument from suffering that we find in Singer: namely, that if we could engineer an animal that could not feel pain, would it then be permissible to abuse it? Nussbaum makes a different argument against the principle of suffering in *Frontiers of Justice*, noting that suffering cannot be said to be a universal negative purely and simply (i.e., suffering is involved in all sorts of processes of learning, accomplishment, and so on—think of the training of a ballerina or classical musician—that in turn may lead to even greater flourishing).

53. Specter, "Test-Tube Burgers," 32–34.

54. Derrida, "Faith and Knowledge," 46.

55. Derrida, "Eating Well," 112.

56. Ibid., 113.

57. James McWilliams, "Eating (Synthetic) Animals," *Atlantic*, last accessed July 23, 2011, http://www.theatlantic.com/food/archive/2010/06/eating-synthetic-animals/58930.

58. Derrida, "Faith and Knowledge," 42. For a powerful, if rapid, indictment of the "ethical carnivore" position of Pollan and others, see Jonathan Safran Foer, *Eating Animals* (New York: Little, Brown, 2009), 214, 256–57.

59. Derrida, "Faith and Knowledge," 50.

60. Ibid., 51–52.

61. Esposito, *Bios*, 116.

62. Specter, "Test-Tube Burgers," 32–33.

63. Teubner, "Dealing with Paradoxes of Law," 58.

64. Ibid.

65. Derrida, "Faith and Knowledge," 25. And he then gives "a single example," namely Carl Schmitt's acknowledgment "that the ostensibly purely political categories to which he resorted were the product of a secularization or of a theologico-political heritage," so that even as he lamented the process of "depoliticization" and the "neutralization of the political"—as, for example, Luhmann would—this was, as Derrida notes, explicitly with reference to "a European legal tradition that in his eyes doubtless remained indissociable from 'our' thought of the political" (25–26). In connection with this discussion of Schmitt, see also Derrida, *The Beast and the Sovereign*, 70–75.

66. For a convincing rejoinder to the reading of Derrida as a fundamentally religious thinker, see chap. 4 of Hägglund, *Radical Atheism*.

67. Derrida, "Faith and Knowledge," 46–47.

68. Ibid., 13.

69. Ibid., 41.

70. Ibid., 55.

71. Derrida, *Rogues*, 155–56.

72. Derrida, "Faith and Knowledge," 43.

73. Leonard Lawlor, *This Is Not Sufficient: An Essay on Animality and Human Nature in Derrida* (New York: Columbia University Press, 2007), 16–17. As Lawlor notes, the texts that occupy Derrida in *Rogues*, *Politics of Friendship*, and "Force of Law"—Husserl's *The Crisis of European Science*, Benjamin's *The Critique of Violence*, Schmitt's *The Concept of the Political*—all date from between the two world wars, and this is no coincidence. "It seems to me," Lawlor writes, "that Derrida focuses on this period, the time between the two world wars, because a world war is *already* a form of globalization; it announces globalization" (17) in its world-encompassing form and in its necessary embrace of technoscience to achieve its objectives (both key components of globalization, and not just in Derrida's analysis).

74. Ibid., 108.

75. Derrida, *Rogues*, 142.

76. Paul Roberts, "Carnivores Like Us," *Seed* (May 15, 2008): last accessed July 23, 2011, http://seedmagazine.com/content/article/carnivores_like_us/P1/.

77. Ibid.

78. Ibid.

79. Derrida, "Faith and Knowledge," 42.

80. Michel Foucault, "Power Affects the Body," in *Foucault Live: Collected Interviews 1961–1984*, ed. Sylvère Lotringer (New York: Semiotexte, 1989), 211.

81. Esposito, *Bios*, 11.

82. Borradori, *Philosophy in a Time of Terror*, 120.

83. Esposito, *Bios*, 194.

84. Foer, *Eating Animals*, 33.

Index

102; and bioengineering, 96–97;
on embodiment, 22–24, 31–34,
37, 48, 58, 102; and immunitary
logic, 37–39, 43, 49–50, 58, 53; on
law, 22–23, 31–32; on the political, 31–35, 50–51, 102, 116n97;
on race, 43; on rights, 22–23; on
sovereignty, 22, 24, 31–33, 48
Francione, Gary, 14
Freud, Sigmund, 66; on origins of law,
9–10, 133n20

genocide: and animals (non-human),
44–46, 49, 104; and fetuses, 47;
and Nazis, 37, 43–44, 102
globalization, 99–104; and factory
farming, 48–50, 51–52, 101–2;
and human rights, 133n22; and
meat, 96, 100–102; and NGOs, 24,
27–28

Hägglund, Martin, 57, 75, 82, 86, 92,
95, 123n21
Hansell, Mike, 77, 128n21
Haraway, Donna, 35, 38
Heidegger, Martin: on animals (nonhuman) as "poor in world," 67,
79, 80, 129n43; on "being-toward-
death," 19, 78; on Dasein, 25,
73–76, 79–82; humanism and,
4–7, 40, 73, 75, 78–82, 107n13,
108n26; on technicity, 3–6, 107n3,
107n11, 108n18, 117n11
Hitler, Adolph, 98
Hobbes, Thomas, 38
Holocaust. See genocide
humanism: in Agamben, 78, 115n77; in
Deleuze, 65–66, 78; in Heidegger,
4–6, 40, 73, 75, 78–82; in Lacan,
64–66; in Žižek, 78
Husserl, Edmund, 73

immunitary logic: Derrida and, 6,
38, 86, 94–95, 98–101, 102–3;

Esposito and, 6, 38–39, 43, 49–50,
55–56, 58–59, 71, 85–86, 90,
98–99, 102; and ethics, 84–86; and
factory farming, 49–52; and law,
90, 92–94, 98–101; and "life,"
38–39, 41, 43, 55–56, 71; and
locavores, 98; and protection of
animals (non-human), 101–5

Jamieson, Dale, 83–84

Kant, Immanuel, 6, 16, 57, 87, 93,
113n30
King, Barbara, 69–70, 77–78, 126n23
Krell, David Farrell, 79, 129n40,
129n43

Lacan, Jacques, 64–66
LaCapra, Dominick, 25–27, 73, 78–79
Latour, Bruno, 83; and political ecology, 88–89
law: and animals (non-human), 11–17,
65–66, 89, 103–5; autopoiesis of,
87–91; vs. biopower, 31–34; as
conditional and performative, 87–
88, 90–93, 94–95, 98–101, 103–4;
Derrida on, 9–10, 16–17, 87–88,
91–95, 97–100, 113n30, 133n20;
Foucault on, 22–23, 31–32; as
immunitary, 90, 92–94, 98–101;
impossible origins of, 8–10, 66–67,
133n20; vs. justice, 87–88, 90–93,
103–4; and Latour's political
ecology, 88–90; Luhmann on,
87–91, 99
Lawlor, Leonard, 100, 136n73
Lazzarato, Maurizio, 31–34, 38, 48, 53
Lemm, Vanessa, 40
Leroi-Gourhan, André, 75–77
Levinas, Emmanuel, 20
"life": antinomies of, 56–59, 63,
73–74, 82, 103, 104, 123n16; and
antinomies of biocentrism, 59–60;
and desire for nonperspectival

"life" (*continued*)
ethics, 85–86; and environmental ethics, 59–60, 83–84; and fetuses, 47–48, 59; and globalization, 100, 102, 133n22; and immunitary logic, 38–39, 41, 43, 55–56, 71, 103, 133n22; and Latour's political ecology, 88–89; and law, 92, 93, 97–98, 133n22; and meat, 96–99; and Nietzsche, 39–42; and synthetic biology, 60–62, 73–74
Liu, Lydia, 66
locavores, 97–98
Luhmann, Niklas, 31; and autopoiesis of law, 87–90, 99; on ethics, 132n18; and immunitary logic, 38, 85–86, 90; and law vs. morality, 88, 90–91
Luke, Tim, 59–60

Maturana, Humberto, 70, 76
meat: animals (non-human) and, 94–98, 100–101, 104–5; and "carnophallogocentrism," 94–99; and globalization, 96; and sovereignty, 95, 97–98, 100–102; synthetic, 94–99

Nealon, Jeffrey, 31–32, 53
Nietzsche, Friedrich, 32, 39–42
Noë, Alva, 69–70
Norris, Andrew, 47, 117n11
Nussbaum, Martha, 96, 135n52

Patton, Paul, 93
Posner, Richard, 13–16, 18, 20, 112n18

Rabinow, Paul, 35
race, and biopolitics, 9, 43, 56, 72, 102, 104
Rancière, Jacques, 24–28, 30, 33
Rasch, William, 90–91, 132n18
Rawls, John, 20
Regan, Tom, 14, 16, 20, 135n52
religion: Derrida on, 9, 92, 94, 98–100;

and ethics, 85, 90–92; and globalization, 99–101; and immunitary logic, 92, 94, 98–100; and law, 92, 94–95, 97–100, 136n65; and "life," 59, 85; and politics of the left, 28–30, 92, 97–100, 116n97
rights: and animals (non-human), 7–8, 11, 13–17, 104, 112n26; Arendt on, 6–8, 6–10, 23, 109n33; Butler on, 114n48; Derrida on, 16, 133n22; Esposito on, 8, 109n33; and fetuses, 47; and globalization, 133n22; Schmitt on, 46–47, 89–90; will-based vs. interest-based theories of, 15–16, 112n26, 135n52
Roberts, Paul, 101
Rorty, Richard, 60, 86, 93
Rose, Nikolas, 35, 51–52
Rosenthal, Robert, 67–68

Sax, Boria, 44
Schmitt, Carl, 24, 46–47, 94–95, 121n17, 136n65
Shelley, Mary, 61
Shukin, Nicole, 51–52
Simondon, Gilbert, 57, 92
Singer, Peter, 11, 14–16, 20, 44, 96, 112n18, 135n52
Sloterdijk, Peter, 4, 40–41
Smith, Hamilton, 61
sovereignty: Agamben on, 5, 24, 32–33, 47, 117n11; and animals (non-human), 65–67, 94–98; Derrida on, 5, 65–66, 94–95, 97–99, 113n30; and fetuses, 47–48; Foucault on, 22, 24, 31–33, 48; and meat, 95, 97–98, 100–102; and the phallus, 94–95, 134n41; as sacrificial, 95, 97–99; Schmitt on, 46–47
Spinoza, Benedict, 59–60, 85
Staten, Henry, 57
Stiegler, Bernard, 75–77, 128n18